SHIPWRECKS
— OF —
MASSACHUSETTS
— BAY —

THOMAS HALL

Charleston — London
THE
History
PRESS

Published by The History Press
Charleston, SC 29403
www.historypress.net

Front cover: *Last Fight of the Speedy, 1804,* Peter Rindlisbacher.

First published 2012

Manufactured in the United States

ISBN 978.1.60949.679.1

Library of Congress CIP data applied for.

*Dedicated to those that go down to the sea in ships
and those that go down to find them.*

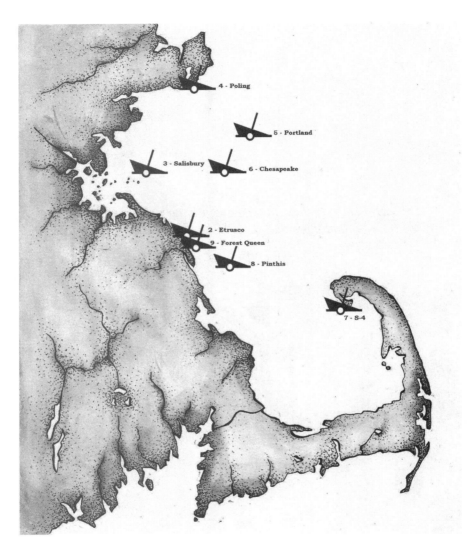

Location of the eight wrecks covered in the book with corresponding chapters.

CONTENTS

INTRODUCTION

There is a granite monument over a mass grave in Wellfleet that reads, "In memory of those brave mariners lost in the wreck of the British ship *Jason* off the back shore of Cape Cod December 5, 1893." The monument lists the names of the twenty-six men lost and one survivor on that fateful day. It was created and funded by the Wellfleet Historical Society as well as several other groups dedicated to the Bicentennial in 1976.

Behind the Congregational Church in Scituate, there is a mass grave marked by a large rock with the inscription "In memory of the sailors wrecked on Egypt Beach 1844. Bodies rest here." This wreck is even more obscure than the *Jason*. In fact, none of the local historians know the names of the boat and crew or the circumstances of its demise. No one in Scituate is related to this unknown wreck filled with sailors lost to history; I suspect no one in Wellfleet is related to those lost on the *Jason*. Still, in both cases, we are touched enough by the tragedy to build a monument.

These types of monuments dot the coastline of Massachusetts Bay. One of the most famous is in Gloucester and reads, "They that go down to the sea in ships (1623–1923)." The inscription is taken from Psalm 107, which reads:

> *They that go down to the sea in ships,*
> *That do business in great waters;*
> *These see the works of the Lord,*
> *And his wonders in the deep.*

Facing out of Gloucester Harbor, the statue shows a helmsman sailing as close hauled to the wind as possible, straining to keep his vessel on course, presumably to clear dangerous rocks. As one of the most active fishing ports in New England over the last four centuries, many families in Gloucester have experienced the pain of losing a relative and friend to the sea. A notable recent example is the *Andrea Gail*, the fishing boat that went down in 1991 and was the subject of the movie *The Perfect Storm*.

I discovered my favorite monument to a mariner's fate when I was researching my first book *The T.W. Lawson: The Fate of the World's Only Seven-Masted Schooner*. On St. Agnes in the Isles of Scilly, southwest England, there is a church with a stained-glass window that reads, "In memory of all those from St. Agnes who put to sea to save the lives of others." Behind this small church there are a number of graves of sailors lost in wrecks and sailors lost trying to save them. There is a mass grave containing those that perished when the *T.W. Lawson* went down, including Billie Cook Hicks, the Trinity House pilot who went aboard the *T.W. Lawson* to get her to safety.

What is it about shipwrecks and the sea that fascinates us? Or reading Edgar Allen Poe and Mary Shelley and going to horror movies? Is it that there is not much that separates a gentle sail along the coast with a terrifying nor'easter blowing us toward the rocks? Wrecks make us wonder if we have what it takes to navigate out of a storm. Are we good enough? Can our boat handle it? Does it matter? When a storm kicks up with huge waves and strong winds or a dense fog blankets a busy channel, is there anything we can do but experience the same brutal and terrifying fate as those before us? Is the psychology that forces us to look at a wreck along the highway and gazelles to watch their own get eaten by a lion the same that moves us to study and dive on shipwrecks?

Psychologists like Carl Jung have studied this question and concluded that if we approach darkness and the macabre in the right way, it can lead to light. Jung would say we find disasters titillating, a weird physiological arousal and an animal stimulation—with evolutionary value. In the case of the gazelles, she watches her fawn getting eaten by a lion and learns what not to do. And some humans might share this trait—when we see or study a wreck and the people onboard, we learn what not to do. But we get more: we get to know ourselves better.

According to Jung, morbid curiosity causes us to think about the meaning of suffering, death and life. Our curiosity with shipwrecks causes us to think about the suffering, death, fear and destruction an angry sea can bring to mariners and their families. But there are other reasons we are fascinated by wrecks. This fascination can be lucrative, as these fateful ships often contain valuable cargo from gold and silver to Chinese porcelain and timber. The

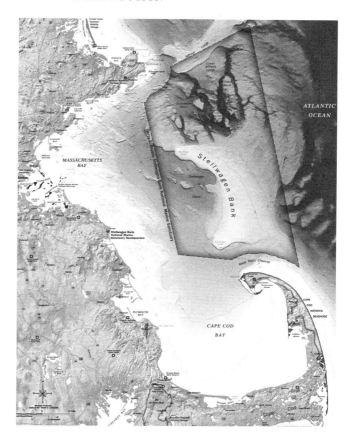

Mass Bay showing
Stellwagen Bank.
Courtesy NOAA.

pursuit of knowledge and artifacts well below the surface is also adventurous, exciting and fun. So we wonder about those that go down to the sea in ships and fail to return; we build monuments to their fate and are fascinated by what lies below the surface.

Held by a distinctive arm along the coast of Massachusetts and extending as far as thirty miles out to sea, Mass Bay covers over eight hundred square miles, making it one of the largest bays in the Atlantic Ocean. The mouth of Mass Bay is guarded in the east by Stellwagen Bank, an underwater plateau stretching nineteen miles from the tip of Cape Cod north and six miles across at its widest point. The bay is enclosed in the west by Boston and its South and North Shores, in the north by Cape Ann and in the south by Cape Cod and includes Boston Harbor, Dorchester Bay, Quincy Bay, Hingham Bay and Cape Cod Bay. This prevalence of bays in Massachusetts, especially when you include the adjacent Narragansett and Buzzards Bays, gives the commonwealth the nickname "The Bay State." It is part of the Gulf of Maine, which reaches from Cape Cod to Nova Scotia. As we will see time and time again, ships entering Mass Bay in a nor'easter are soon trapped deep inside its labyrinth, embraced by the arm of Cape Cod and neck of Cape Ann and pushed onto the rocky lee shores by the wind and waves.

According to the National Oceanic and Atmospheric Administration (NOAA), Ice Age glaciers began retreating from eastern Massachusetts around eighteen thousand years ago, leaving portions of Stellwagen Bank dry and home to grasses, forests and animals. It is likely around twelve thousand years ago that Native Americans inhabited these areas and exploited the rich marine resources found along the shore. Rising sea levels slowly inundated Mass Bay, pushing the native populations to settlements along the current shoreline. Prior to the arrival of Europeans on the eastern shores of New England possibly as early as the sixteenth century, the area around Mass Bay was the territory of several Algonquin-speaking tribes, including the Massachusetts, Nauset and Wampanoag

The sloping sides of Stellwagen Bank cause deepwater currents to rise, bringing nutrients and minerals from the bottom, feeding a rich ecosystem including Atlantic cod, silver hake, yellow tail flounder, blue fin and yellow fin tuna, striped bass, blue fish and numerous species of shark. Shellfish, such as lobster, sea scallops, squid and ocean quahogs, are also prevalent. Many marine birds and mammals such as seals, dolphins and porpoises call the bank home, as do reptiles such as the Leatherback sea turtle. Whale watchers can frequently see humpback, minke and fin whales and, one of the most critically endangered whale species, the North Atlantic right whale.

Early in the seventeenth century, a variety of European explorers, including Samuel de Champlain and John Smith, charted the area. Plans for the first permanent British settlements on the east coast of North America began in 1606. King James I of England formed the Plymouth Company to settle the northern areas of the new world, including present-day New England. Though many of the early settlements were difficult and eventually abandoned, English ships continued to come to New England to fish and trade with the Indians. From time to time, these ships wrecked.

In November 1620, a group of Pilgrims seeking to escape religious persecution by English authorities crossed the Atlantic, landing first in present-day Provincetown and, finding no suitable land to farm, crossed the bay and established Plymouth Colony. Although Plymouth faced great hardships and earned few profits, it enjoyed a positive reputation in England, and its reports encouraged further immigration. Edward Winslow and William Bradford, two of its leaders, published an account of their adventures called *Mourt's Relation* in 1622. In 1624, a small fishing village at Cape Ann, near present-day Gloucester, was established. Though not profitable, it sowed the seeds of further expansion around Mass Bay.

In the early years, the colony was highly dependent on imports from England and the investments of a number of wealthy immigrants. Certain businesses quickly started, notably shipbuilding, fisheries and the fur and lumber trades. As early as 1632, ships built in the colony began trading, either with other colonies, England or foreign ports in Europe. By 1660, its merchant fleet was estimated to contain over two hundred ships, and by the end of the century, its shipyards were estimated to turn out several hundred ships annually. In the early years, the fleet primarily carried fish from the West Indies to Europe. It was common for a merchant to ship dried fish to Portugal or Spain, pick up wine and oil for transport to England and then carry finished goods from England or elsewhere back to New England.

Colonial authorities in Mass Bay opposed attempts by England to control fishing and trading routes, for example, with the Navigation Acts of 1651. The colony's economy depended on the success of its trade, in part because its land was not as suitable for agriculture as that of other colonies like Virginia, where large plantations could be established. Fishing was important enough that those involved in it were exempted from taxation and military service. As technology progressed, fishing vessels and fishing methods evolved to meet the demands of the market. The small, rowed craft of the colonial period were replaced by swift schooners in the eighteenth and nineteenth centuries, which were then replaced by engine driven trawlers in the twentieth century.

Whaling also played an important role in the maritime heritage of New England. In the late 1500s, whalers from Spain came to New England, possibly as far south as Stellwagen Bank, but it was not until the seventeenth century that shore-based whaling became a common activity along the East Coast. Small boats set out from the shores of Cape Cod in pursuit of right whales. Once harpooned, the whales were killed with a lance and then towed ashore, where their blubber was rendered into oil. During the eighteenth and nineteenth centuries, larger whale ships departed from Massachusetts ports for whaling grounds far offshore. As whale populations diminished in the Atlantic Ocean, Massachusetts whalers rounded Cape Horn into the Pacific Ocean to find more whales. The whaler *Essex* took this route and was the basis for *Moby Dick*.

As the largest American city closest to Europe, Boston became a destination for many immigrants. Though travel by sail was dangerous, passenger traffic across Mass Bay steadily built from the seventeenth to the nineteenth century as New England's economy and population grew. Prior to establishment of regularly scheduled sailing packets, early nineteenth-century travelers may have waited weeks for their vessels to fill their holds or their cabins. Once started, these trips usually took six weeks or longer, turning even the fastest vessels in to maritime prisons when the wind stopped blowing. During the nineteenth century, steam propulsion dramatically transformed passenger travel; passengers could now plan on a departure time, journey length and comforts like lavish meals and warm beds. Today, thousands of people cross Massachusetts Bay on high-speed ferries that connect Cape Cod to Boston and on cruise ships that depart Boston for Bermuda, the Caribbean, Canada and the New England coast.

The waters of Mass Bay have also been the scene of conflict several times over the past three centuries. From the Revolutionary War to the War of 1812 to World War II, war ships, privateers, rumrunners and submarines all navigated and fought in these waters.

In 1854, the U.S. Coast Survey sent Lieutenant Commander Henry Stellwagen to survey and chart the bank between Cape Cod and Cape Ann. Prior to Stellwagen's survey, it was believed there were two small banks in the area: one just to the north of Cape Cod, and one in the middle of the entrance to Mass Bay. He showed that they were part of one large bank; as a result, navigation was vastly improved and the bank was named after him in 1855. At that same time, ships like the *Forest Queen* were passing over the bank and in to Mass Bay on their way back from the opium trade in China, carrying silk, porcelain and, it was believed, silver ingots.

After the Civil War, New England's merchants focused on shipping bulk commodities along the coast, primarily on fore- and aft-rigged schooners. A common route would have cargos of granite and ice departing Mass Bay and returning with coal and lumber.

During Prohibition, many entrepreneurs converted a variety of vessels so they could smuggle liquor. This lucrative, albeit illegal, rumrunning involved anchoring larger vessels in Mass Bay and transferring the alcohol into smaller craft that would carry the contraband to shore. In October 1924, the United States Coast Guard squadron based in Boston discovered more than a dozen vessels waiting on Stellwagen Bank to have their illegal cargos offloaded. After some resistance, they captured the smugglers and their vessels but not before 850 cases of brandy, champagne and whiskey were tossed overboard. This scene repeated itself several times throughout the 1920s since the shallow water over Stellwagen Bank was an ideal place to anchor.

INTRODUCTION

View of Boston Harbor, 1906. Note the mix of sail and steam vessels in the harbor and a paddlewheel vessel similar to the *Portland* along the pier. *Courtesy Library of Congress.*

Established in 1992, the Stellwagen Bank National Marine Sanctuary is an 842-square-mile area of ocean managed by NOAA with its administrative office located on First Cliff in Scituate, Massachusetts, which used to house the U.S. Coast Guard station. Today, fishermen travel from their home ports to Stellwagen Bank, the heart of the sanctuary, to harvest finfish and shellfish; container ships, tankers, tugs and barges pass over the bank on their way to Boston; and sailboats, cruisers, scuba divers, researchers, whales, fish and tourists on ferries enjoy the bay on the surface and deep below.

This book is about shipwrecks in Mass Bay. Eight shipwrecks will be discussed in depth, with newly updated research; many other wrecks will be discussed briefly as they relate to the particular location. These core wrecks were selected because they exemplify the key factors in a shipwreck: technology, ship design and weather. In the two centuries from the *Shannon-Chesapeake* battle in 1813 to today, shipbuilding has gone through enormous advances, from wooden schooners and ships to today's massive steel tankers. In this period, there were also enormous advances in how we forecast weather—always the critical factor in any wreck—from simple barometers and the telegraph to global positioning systems and radar.

In some of these wrecks, all aboard perished. The loss of the *Portland* and 192 of its crew and passengers in the 1898 *Portland* Gale coupled with the loss of many more on land is one example. In some cases, all survived. The loss of the *Forest Queen* in a nor'easter in 1853 when all the crew and passengers were saved is another example. The *Forest Queen* however, represents another aspect of what fascinates us with shipwrecks—treasure. Returning home from years in the China Trade, it was believed she was carrying a vast amount of silver ingots.

The wrecks I selected also exemplify two other key factors in a shipwreck: human error and bad luck. The *Pinthis* went down with the loss of all onboard. Why didn't the ship that hit them call for help immediately? Why were they going so fast in fog? The answers remain a mystery. We will discuss the collision of the submarine *S-4* with a Coast Guard ship—certainly a case where both parties, as professional mariners, should have been more prudent. The *Etrusco* was turned away in a storm by a Boston Harbor pilot, only to be blown on to the South Shore where it remained beached and gawked at by tourists for nine months. The *Chester A. Poling*, a modern tanker, broke apart in the mouth of Gloucester Harbor, within sight of safety. And finally, the *City of Salisbury*, filled with exotic zoo animals and thus named the "Zoo Ship," went down in the shadow of Graves Light in Boston Harbor using an inaccurate chart. If not for poor decisions and misfortune, these shipwrecks could have been avoided.

The last wreck chosen is not technically a wreck—that is, the ships involved did not sink or run aground. However, it was an important battle during the War of 1812 between the HMS *Shannon* and the USS *Chesapeake* that caused the deaths of many sailors, including the captain of the *Chesapeake*. Mortally wounded, Captain Lawrence uttered the famous words, "Tell the men to fire faster and don't give up the ship!" This phrase was adopted by Oliver Hazard Perry and the young U.S. Navy. Viewed by many along the coast, this battle represents a turning point in the birth of the navy and the history of Mass Bay. It also represents a case where ships were wrecked on purpose.

The wrecks were selected and the chapters arranged so that as you sail around the bay, you can study these wrecks along your route. We start out in Scituate with the *Etrusco* (1956), head north to Boston Harbor and the *City of Salisbury* (1938), turn clockwise toward Gloucester and the *Chester A. Poling* (1977), head south to the *Portland* (1898) and *Shannon-Chesapeake* Battle (1813), to Provincetown and the submarine *S-4* (1927), head west to the *Pinthis* (1930) and return to Scituate and the *Forest Queen* (1853). As we venture around Mass Bay, we will also discuss other wrecks when they add perspective. These eight instructive wrecks, however, will give you a chance, as you pass by them, to imagine the state of the weather, technology on the ship, type of ship and condition of the crew and passengers. It will also give you a chance to instruct your own crew, particularly those new to the bay, as to a particular shipwreck and what not to do.

I have been diving all my life, mostly along the coast of Mass Bay and the eastern United States but also in England, Greece and the Philippines. I couple this enjoyment of diving with a thirst for historical perspective. As many divers do, I always imagine the circumstances that led to the wreck—the weather, the ship and the crew—and try to fill in the blanks with sound research. That was my approach with the *T.W. Lawson*. I dove on her over twenty times, interviewed survivor's relatives, searched through historical societies and museums and pieced the story together. The result was my book *The* T.W. Lawson: *The Fate of the World's Only Seven-Masted Schooner*, published in 2003 and updated in 2006 by The History Press, the same group publishing this book. The point has always been to increase knowledge of the subject—to advance the ball—not to claim to be the absolute and sole authority on a particular wreck. Many excellent divers and historians have studied the wrecks covered in this book, and many more will come after. There are always new discoveries to be made and new technologies to help us get there.

The research approach with this book was twofold: pouring through historical archives and talking with survivors or survivors' families when possible and combing over the sight of the wreck myself, whether on shore or in the deep, or interviewing those that have. When possible, I dove directly on these wrecks or scoured the shoreline where they went aground. Some wrecks, like the *Portland*, are in water too deep to safely dive. I was able to get down to the *City of Salisbury*, *Chester A. Poling*, *Pinthis* and *Forest Queen*, have stood on the shore where the *Etrusco* and *Jason* rested and sailed over where the *Paulding* and *S-4* collided. I coupled this direct research with discussions with many other divers who also went down on the wrecks, most notably Bill Carter and Tom Mulloy.

No discussion of wrecks in Mass Bay can be complete without including renowned wreck diver Bill Carter. Not only a tenacious and professional wreck diver, he also shared the history and significance of the vessels with communities that may have long forgotten them. According to Bill Carter's son Bryan, his father's passion for diving began in the 1950s when he was in college, after he read an article about Jacques Cousteau's Aqua-Lung. With some money from an inheritance, Carter bought his first scuba set-up and ended up meeting Brad Luther, known as the "grandfather of New England wreck diving."

"Brad got him hooked on wreck diving and archaeology and that was it," Bryan said, adding that a lot of Carter's early diving was done with well-known Rockport historian and family friend Paul Sherman. Sometime in the 1960s, Bryan said his father bought the first Avon inflatable sold in New England and later that decade traded it in for a sixteen-foot Sea Ray and named it *Wreckhunter*. "He found new wrecks with this boat, including the *Albert Gallatin* off the coast of Manchester, Mass," Bryan said.

Through the years, Carter was able to upgrade his boat with the latest technology, with which he was able to locate the wreck of the *Kiowa* three miles off Boston Light. According to Bryan, his father was a cautious and conservative diver who instilled these traits in his sons and other divers, notably Tom Mulloy, another well-known diver, friend and diving buddy of Carter's.

"Bill and his boys, along with Brian Skerry, were about to anchor into the wreck when I came up from my dive," Mulloy said. "They asked if I was diving alone, to which I said I was never alone—I had Kristal, my golden retriever on board. Bill invited me to dive with him and the boys the next weekend and we dove on countless wrecks up and down the coast." Though he had been diving for twenty years before he met Carter, Mulloy said his knowledge of local wrecks was very limited. A few of the wrecks Mulloy dove with Carter include *Kiowa* off Ultonia Ridge, *Albert Gallatin* off Manchester, *City of Salisbury* and USS *New Hampshire* near Graves Light, *Delaware* off Minot's Ledge, *Chester A. Poling* off Gloucester and *Aransas* off Chatham. His favorite was the *Pinthis* off Scituate.

"The story of the sinking fascinated him. In 1990, we were fortunate to have the captain's granddaughter visit for the weekend and come out with us to lay a wreath on the site for the sixtieth anniversary of the sinking," said Bryan, mentioning how important the *Pinthis* whistle was to his father. "As Dad, Rusty and I were lifting it over the side of our sixteen-foot boat, it was filled with mud and weighed several hundred pounds," Bryan said. "We wrestled it over the side but lost our grip as we were putting it down on the deck. It dropped about four inches and put a foot-long crack through the hull of the boat. Fortunately, it was a slow leak and the team made it safely back to shore where the boat was repaired." Bryan recalls that in order to keep his many young grandchildren from touching the whistle once it was cleaned and polished, Carter made up a story that Casper the ghost lived way up inside and that if the grandchildren touched it, they would wake him up!

A decade ago, Carter, well into his seventies, stopped diving and shifted his focus to sharing his knowledge. He was instrumental in establishing some of the exhibits at the Maritime & Irish Mossing Museum in Scituate, Massachusetts. The pride of Bill's collection is the whistle from the tanker *Pinthis*. Other favorites include fifty portholes brought up from the *Angela*, the telegraph from the *Mars*, the copper spikes hand wrought in Paul Revere's foundry and dead eyes retrieved from the USS *New Hampshire* and ornate brass fittings from the *Aransas*. It was at this time that I met Bill. He willingly shared stories of his wreck dives, especially the *Pinthis*, *City of Salisbury* and *Forest Queen*. It was with the *Forest Queen* that I learned the most from Bill, as well as Tom Mulloy, who discovered the wreck in 1991. In 2005, the same diving crew that dove on the *T.W. Lawson* with me in England came to Scituate to dive and research the *Forest Queen*. Other diving groups have made significant contributions to our understanding and enjoyment of wrecks in Mass Bay, such as Boston Deep Diving, Boston Sea Rovers and MetroWest Dive Club.

Along with diving and talking with other divers, I poured through historical archives and talked with survivors or survivor's families when possible. One example of this type of primary research occurred in 2005 when I flew to Genoa, Italy, to interview Giovanni Belfiore, one of the last surviving crewmembers of the 1956 wreck of the *Etrusco*, and to Sarasota, Florida, to talk with Jim Howard, who handled all the radio communications during the rescue of the crew. When direct interviews were not possible, I relied on historical archives. Numerous documents can be found in the many local museums and archives, such as the Massachusetts Archives in Boston and Peabody Essex Museum, as well as historical newspaper accounts. Historical Societies along the coast from Gloucester to Wellfleet also have a wealth of information on these wrecks. Finally, NOAA has extensive information on wrecks in Mass Bay, particularly in the Stellwagen Bank area that it manages.

There are many books on wrecks I found valuable, such as *New England's Legacy of Ships*, by Henry Keatts (American Merchant Marine Museum Press, 1988); *Gifts from the Celestial Kingdom*, by Thomas Layton (Stanford University Press, 2002); *The Perfect Storm*, by Sebastian Junger (Norton and Company, 1997); and a number of entertaining books by Robert Ellis Cahill, such as *Shipwrecks and Treasures* and *Strange Sea Sagas* (Chandler-Smith Publishing House, 1984). Dave Ball and Fred Freitas researched and wrote definitive reports on the *Etrusco* (1995), *Portland* Gale (1995) and *Fairfax-Pinthis* disaster (1997). An excellent account of fishing in Mass Bay over the past fifty years can be found in the recently published book by Skip DeBrusk called *Codfish, Dogfish, Mermaids and Frank* (Reginald vanWenwick Press, 2007). However excellent these and other books are, one cannot get a complete picture of the wrecks in New England without reading the myriad of books by Edward Rowe Snow.

Born in Winthrop in 1902, Snow is widely known for his stories of New England coastal history, pirates and other nautical subjects. He was the author of more than one hundred publications, including *The Islands of Boston Harbor*. With this publication in 1935 and for the next forty years, he gained fame as a historian, storyteller, lecturer, preservationist and treasure hunter. He is also well known for carrying on the tradition of the Flying Santa from 1936 to 1980. Every Christmas, he would hire a small plane and drop wrapped gifts to the lighthouse keepers and their families. Many credit him with saving Fort Warren, located on Georges Island, in the 1950s.

Many also credit him with stretching the truth and telling tall tales. While this makes for an interesting story, it could throw a researcher off the path from fact to embellishment. Two examples come to mind. Although never proven, he always claimed to be a relative of Edward Rowe, engineer of the *T.W. Lawson* and one of two survivors of the famous wreck. A more famous example occurred with the *Portland*, which, according to Snow, was located and dove on in the last week of June 1945. Snow records the affidavit of diver Al George in his book *Strange Tales from Nova Scotia to Cape Hatteras*. According to the affidavit, George found the site by traveling to a location discovered by Captain Charles G. Carver of Rockland, Maine, identified as "Highland Light bears 175 degrees true at a distance of 4.5 miles; the Pilgrim Monument, 6.25 miles away has a bearing of 210 degrees; Race Point Coast Guard Station, bearing 255 degrees, is seven miles distant." Snow had a plaque dedicated in Provincetown to the sailors who lost their lives. While most were sympathetic to honoring those lost at sea, they were also skeptical of Snow finding the location of the ship. We now know, based on work completed in the last decade by NOAA identifying and scanning the wreck, that Snow had the location wrong.

Despite skepticism by some, Snow's body of work on maritime activities in Mass Bay contributed enormously to our knowledge of these wrecks and preservation of historic sites. My two favorite books by Snow are *Storms and Shipwrecks of New England* and *The Lighthouses of New England*, recently updated by Commonwealth Editions in 2002. Since these books by Snow were originally published in 1943 and 1945, I found the updates by Jeremy D'Entremont to be important and well researched. In the last ten years, even more has been learned—further advancing the ball. In particular, we have included in this book important new information on the *Portland*, *Shannon-Chesapeake*, *Etrusco*, *Pinthis* and *Forest Queen* wrecks.

I would like to thank the many maritime experts who contributed to my understanding, such as Dave Ball, Fred Freitas and Mat Brown with the Scituate Historical Society; Matt Lawrence, maritime archeologist at NOAA Stellwagen Bank; divers Tom Mulloy and Bill Carter; Willy Bemis, director of Shoals Marine Lab; and Alec Collyer, BBC UK underwater videographer. I thank my dive buddies Chris Silva, my daughter and master diver Chloe Hall, Billy Fenton (EOD, USN Ret), Mark Brandon, and my brother Larry Hall who dove with and supported me on numerous wreck dives. I also thank the North Atlantic Scuba dive shop in Marshfield, Mass, for their support, training and advice. And finally to my father, Steve Hall, dive buddy emeritus, for teaching me the craft thirty-five years ago and encouraging me to write this book.

Many of these wrecks were also researched by students during a course I taught at Emmanuel College in 2011 called Wrecks, Legends, Storms and Opium along the New England Coast, and I thank them for their hard work and dedication. I also thank Peg Patten, owner of the Front Street Book Store in Scituate, for her fine editing and encouragement. To bring the stories to life, I have included many photographs that were found in the myriad of historical societies, maritime museums, and private collections around New England. When they did not exist, Michelle Garcia, a wonderful maritime illustrator, brought them to life and for that I thank her. Finally, I thank my entire family, in particular my wife, Cathy; daughter Nicole; and mother, Marge, for their support and time reviewing the text and design of this book.

CHAPTER 1

ETRUSCO

OLD SCITUATE LIGHT

42° 12.18 N
70° 42.57 W

O ur tour begins at the base of Old Scituate Light at the entrance to Scituate Harbor where a plaque reads "The Italian freighter Etrusco, a 7000 ton Liberty ship, grounded here March 16, 1956, in a northeast blizzard. All hands safe. Refloated November 22, 1956."

Built in 1811, Scituate Light is the oldest lighthouse complex in North America if you consider the original keeper's house, light and other buildings together. In its two centuries of service, it has gone from a stubby lighthouse extended to nearly double its height and from complete disrepair to its present state as one of two maritime gems in Scituate. Lawson Tower—the most photographed tower in the world—is the other and clear landmark for many mariners around Mass Bay. Scituate Light was also the scene of one of the most unlikely American victories in the War of 1812, when the two quick-witted women turned back a British raiding party from the HMS *Bulwark*. To their horror, Rebecca and Abigail Bates saw two longboats filled with British soldiers approaching the harbor. With their father, the lighthouse keeper, away, the girls ran to get a pipe and a drum, concealed themselves behind sand dunes and began playing military march music. As the boats drew near shore, the music grew louder and the British, worried American soldiers were ready to defend the harbor, turned and rowed away. Decades later, a local woman recalled asking militia members what happened. "You'll never believe it," they told her. "The British were driven away by two girls playing a fife and drum."

Scituate Light's illumination and therefore function as a nighttime navigation aid was replaced by Minot's Light to the north in 1860. In 1916, when the federal government was ready to auction off the building, a Scituate selectman sent his wife to Boston with a $1,000 check in town funds to buy the light station for the town. Its lantern room was restored in 1930 when a surrounding park was created. It survived the burning of Scituate Harbor by the British in the War of 1812, its decommissioning just before the Civil War, its sale at public auction in 1916 and, in 1956 when a winter storm "parallel parked" the 441-foot Italian freighter *Etrusco* next to the light station, a flood of tourists from around the state.

The story of the *Etrusco* starts in 1942 with the laying of the keel of *Fort Poplar* and ends with her being scrapped in Hong Kong in 1964, eight years after being renamed the SS *Scituate*. During her twenty-two-year life, she survived so-called "crews from hell," action in Normandy and the Gulf of Tonkin and grounding in Scituate. According to Dave Ball and Fred Freitas, who wrote the definitive book on the ship called *From Cradle to Grave—Etrusco!*, her luck, if it can be called that, had just run out.

To understand the *Etrusco*, we must first put it in the context of the time— that is, World War II and England's desperate cry for ships. During the early 1940s, England endured nightly air raids, large losses on the sea from U-boat attacks and the threat of a German land invasion. There were shortages of petroleum, metals and food, particularly wheat. Prior to the war, England operated the largest merchant marine fleet in the world, with 3,000 ocean-going vessels and 1,000 coasters, with half of them at sea at any time bringing in food and materials. Only 165 Royal Navy destroyers were available to protect these merchant ships and this was proving to be a losing battle.

To help Britain rebuild its merchant fleet, U.S. and Canadian shipyards stepped in. Built primarily in Portland, Maine, American Ocean–type ships were of British design but often welded together rather than riveted, which was faster and easier. Each ship's name began with "Ocean"; for example, *Ocean Vanguard* launched in the summer of 1941. In Canada, these ships were riveted and named after Canadian forts to distinguish them from American vessels of similar design; for example, the ship *Fort Poplar*, which later became the *Etrusco*. Of note, these Fort-type ships burned coal; a later version of the ship design burned oil and was categorized as a Victory ship.

The shipbuilding program that mirrored the Ocean and Fort programs for American rather than British use was the Liberty ship program. This shipbuilding effort became so massive that it eventually overshadowed the programs developed to supply the British. However, it is important to note, according to Ball and Freitas, that these Ocean and Fort ships were prototypes to the Liberty ships with a couple modifications, such as a single deckhouse amidships, better crew berthing and water-tube boilers to allow for the efficient use of oil. The combined Ocean, Fort and Liberty programs of the United States and Canada were successful, delivering over three thousand ships. Speaking in the fall of 1943, President Roosevelt stated:

> *The civilian industry has delivered on or ahead of schedule, every ton of every ship they were called upon to build. They have smashed every production quota set for the them, so that today, less than two years after our entry in to the war, the total deadweight tonnage of their ships more than double that of the entire American marine before Pearl Harbor. By the end of 1944, new ships delivered by American yards will equal the combined prewar merchant fleets of the US, Great Britain, Germany, Japan, and Norway.*

These ships carried food, troops and materiel east to aid Europe in large quantities; for example, each ship could carry 440 light tanks or 2,800 jeeps.

When the *Fort Poplar* grounded in Scituate under the new name *Etrusco*, it was widely reported and put on plaques that she was an American-built Liberty ship. In fact, the *Fort Poplar* was built in Vancouver, Canada, by the Burrard Dry Dock Company. The keel was laid June 19, 1942, completed and launched 134 days later, on Halloween Day. The length of the ship was 441 feet overall with a beam of 57 feet and drew two inches shy of 27 feet. She had a deadweight of 10,490 tons, gross tonnage of 7,134 and a displacement of 14,250 long tons. Her navigation equipment was bare bones and included a standard compass, sounding machine, signal lamps and flags, voice tubes from the bridge to the engine room and bells and gongs. The key to understanding how the *Etrusco* grounded centers on her underpowered engine.

All Liberty, Fort and Ocean-type vessels had identical propulsion, that is, a triple-expansion steam engine delivering 2,500 horsepower. The engine was simple and easy to operate, standing as tall as a basketball hoop, weighing 135 tons. Supplying 220 pounds per square inch (psi) of steam to the engine were three Scotch boilers burning coal. The ship carried 2,400 tons of coal and consumed 30 tons a day. Driving a single screw, this engine would push the *Fort Poplar* at a maximum of eleven knots. As we will see, while the upside of the shipbuilding program was a lot of ships built quickly—a major factor in winning the war—a major downside was that these ships were underpowered. An analogy told to me by a marine engineer was that sailing these ships, especially in heavy seas, was like driving an old Volkswagen Beetle filled with people up a steep mountain, say Mount Washington! In ballast and heavy weather—a light weight versus displacement—it was worse as she sat high in the water with the propeller exposed. Now give our Volkswagen a flat tire or two, continue up and down Mount Washington and you have an idea how hard it was to control and make way.

The United States recognized this deficiency with the next generation of cargo ships, the Victory ships. These were a little larger than the Liberty, Ocean and Fort ships, less Spartan and more powerful. Instead of the 2,500 horsepower triple-expansion reciprocating engine, each had a 6,000 horsepower cross-compound steam turbine geared to the propeller axis. This raised the speed from 11.0 knots to 15.5 knots, lessening the danger from submarine attack and improving handling in heavy weather. Unfortunately, this power increase came too late for the *Fort Poplar-Etrusco*, and it would pay a price fourteen years after launching.

After a strong record of service in World War II, including participating in the Invasion of Normandy in 1944, the *Fort Poplar* went into hiding. England's Ministry of Transportation holds no voyage records for her after June 1945, although there is indication she was in Nova Scotia in 1946. On September 29, 1947, the ship reached Mobile, Alabama, and was turned over to the Reserve Fleet, where she remained until Saint Patrick's Day 1948 when she was turned over to new agents and subsequently sold to L'Italica Di Navigazione of Genoa, Italy, and renamed *Etrusco*. For eight years, she carried cargo along the coast of Europe and to the United States.

The *Etrusco* departed for Boston from Emden, Germany, in late February 1956 in ballast—that is, carrying no significant cargo. This was not uncommon even nine years after the war—Europe was not producing enough yet to export and relied on imports from the United States as it continued to rebuild. As we discussed earlier, these types of ships did not sail well lightly loaded, a condition that was well known to the thirty-man Italian crew. Whether their captain, Gaetano Traini, who had just received his master papers and was on his first command, had reservations is not known. The trip across the Atlantic went smoothly, according to Giovanni, and the ship was on schedule, despite a slight detour to the Azores to drop off a sick crewman. The *Etrusco* was scheduled to arrive on the sixteenth of March at Castle Island berth 12 in South Boston to load grain and head back to Europe. The winter in Boston had not been particularly severe, and citizens were looking forward to a warm spring. Little did they know that the first of five major storms was brewing.

The *Etrusco* arrived off Boston Harbor in the early afternoon of March 16 in a growing snowstorm. She was advised by her agent, J.F. Moran Co., that it was not possible to enter the harbor due to poor visibility caused by blowing snow and rough seas. Captain Traini was advised to seek refuge in the lee of Cape Cod. Exactly where the *Etrusco* was between the time she turned from Boston Harbor until grounded off Scituate is not known. Newspaper accounts later reported the captain saw a light, possible Minot's, and a crewmember reported hearing a foghorn. By late afternoon, the storm's intensity had increased into a so-called meteorological bomb. Visibility was zero, the temperature hovered near twenty degrees and winds gusted to eighty miles per hour. At 8:10 p.m., a distress call was received at the Marshfield Coast Guard Radio Station from the *Etrusco*, position unknown, possibly off Plymouth.

In 2005, I flew to Genoa to interview Giovanni Belfiore, a nineteen-year-old cadet officer at the time of the wreck and the youngest member of the crew. Now nearly seventy, with his daughter at his side to translate between English and Italian, he was one of two surviving crewmembers. Giovanni and I explored many aspects of the grounding, including its whereabouts from the afternoon until the grounding that evening. According to Giovanni, the ship turned around at the mouth of Boston Harbor, obviously distressed and angry at not being allowed in. Apparently, the storm, coupled with a lack of qualified pilots, made it too dangerous to wait it out there. So the crew turned east and headed out to sea. Unfortunately, as they were in ballast with snow and ice accumulating on the ship's decks, they were not able to make way against the rough seas and winds of a classic nor'easter. According to Giovanni, they were unable to keep their bow pointed into the wind and waves, lost control and drifted down toward Scituate Light.

At 8:20 p.m. on the sixteenth, Anna Howland of Scituate called the U.S. Coast Guard Station at Scituate informing them that a ship "as big as the *Queen Mary*" was coming ashore at Scituate Light. Her husband, Charles Howland, also spotted the lights of a ship and ran to the beach. A brief break in the driving snow revealed lights of the *Etrusco* about three hundred yards offshore and in trouble. Using flashlights, Howland tried to contact the ship to no avail. Soon after, Bos'n William Miller of the Coast Guard arrived to take command and reported a large vessel two hundred yards off the beach and "apparently pounding badly on the rocks."

An hour and a half after the *Etrusco* was spotted close to shore, Point Allerton Hull Lifeboat Station arrived and preparations were made to set up a modified Lyle gun, a device that shoots lightweight line. With rescue

Etrusco parallel parked next to Old Scituate Light, March 17, 1956. *Courtesty Scituate Historical Society.*

Etrusco high and dry on Cedar Point, Scituate, several days after grounding. *Courtesty Scituate Historical Society.*

lines across the *Etrusco* and more rescue personnel and equipment arriving, a temporary headquarters became necessary. Lina Russo offered her home, which was on the shore directly in front of the beached ship. Soon she was providing hot coffee and food to the cold rescuers and eventually to the crewmembers as they came off the ship. Even though the rescuers tracked snow and oil leaking from the ship in to her home, she never complained. Interestingly, it had been rumored that Lina was from the same Italian village as the crew of the *Etrusco* and spoke the same Italian dialect. In fact, according to Giovanni, this was the not the case. While the crew was primarily from Genoa, Lina Russo's heritage was farther south, near Naples. Regardless, her hospitality was welcomed by all, and she was able to translate.

A communications truck was requested, though owing to the snow, it was unable to arrive on the scene until the early morning of the seventeenth. Fortunately, Scituate had appropriated funds the prior year for upgraded equipment such as pumps, lights and generators, which were utilized throughout the night. Civil Defense operator Jim Howard, at nineteen, the same age as Giovanni, who was still on the stranded *Etrusco*, arrived on the scene to provide a radio link between the Russo home and the Scituate Coast Guard station. Jim spent the night and most of the next day at the Russo home working his radio equipment, connected to Wayne Kestilla at the Coast Guard Station. According to Kestilla, all the Coast Guard communications equipment had failed owing to a power surge. He was able to fix the problem with some Yankee ingenuity—he inserted aluminum foil from a cigarette pack into the back of a problem fuse.

The performance of the Coast Guard during the rescue has been brought into question. Its reaction was slow and equipment in sorry shape. Without the aid of local ham radio operators like Jim Howard and the work of the Scituate Fire Department, which provided, among other things, emergency lighting on the beach, the crew may not have been rescued as successfully as they were. According to Jim, although Bos'n Miller performed well, the criticism overall was justified. Its performance was hindered by two events. The sixteenth was Friday night of Saint Patrick's Day weekend, and many of the guardsmen had been celebrating. But more importantly, in the postwar years, funding for the Coast Guard had been drastically cut, causing degradation in overall readiness. It was fortunate local radio operators like Jim were able to step in and assist.

Before midnight, the engine room of the *Etrusco* began to flood, reaching a height of five feet. To reduce the risk of an explosion, Captain Traini opened the ship's whistle to bleed off the remaining steam, which also stopped power generation, throwing the ship into darkness. According to Giovanni, the inky ship coupled with the howling wind and driving snow was the most frightening thing he and his mates had ever experienced. Concern now centered on the possibility that the crew might try to leave the ship, possibly on lifeboats. They may have been close to doing just that. In September, when power was restored to the *Etrusco* in preparation to get her off the beach, the first sound heard was the abandon ship whistle. When asked about this fifty years later, Giovanni was adamant that the crew was never going to abandon the ship in lifeboats. Owing to the severe wind chill,

Crewmember rescued by breeches buoy on the morning of St. Patrick's Day, March 17, 1956. *Courtesty Scituate Historical Society.*

blowing snow and sand, surging seawater and leaking oil—it is estimated that nearly 180 tons of oil leaked out on the beach through the holes in the hull—Bos'n Miller decided to wait until daybreak to begin bringing crewmembers off the ship. The four hundred or so reporters and sightseers watching would have to wait three or four hours for the big event to begin.

The Scituate Lifeboat Report entries for Saturday morning were as follows:

5:10 am   *Crew commenced laying out hawser and whips*
5:35 am   *Coast Guard cutter Evergreen arrived off Scituate entrance*
5:50 am   *Preparations completed; fired projectile across amidships of Etrusco*
6:00 am   *Hawser secured to Etrusco mast and preparations made to remove men*
6:05 am   *First man removed from Etrusco*

The first man removed by breeches buoy was Gaetano Marcelling, selected because he could speak English. As he approached his rescuers, he asked, "Where are we?" When interviewed later about when the crew first realized they were in trouble, he replied, "I think it was about 2:00 p.m. yesterday. It was white all around us, snow and spray, and we lost our bearings. The pilot at Boston said he could not come to our ship because of the storm. We were past the Boston Light, and the port master said we should return to Cape Cod and anchor. But what could we do? We saw nothing. We could hear nothing."

As the weather continued to improve, justifying Bos'n Miller's decision to wait until daybreak, crewmembers were removed one by one. Captain Traini was the twenty-eighth crewmember off the ship, leaving two crewmembers behind to prevent a technical salvage claim by unauthorized persons. Miller however overruled this move and removed the final two safely at 7:45 a.m. Each of the Italian crewmembers was taken to the Russo home. Interestingly, according to Ball and Freitas, Miller allowed four crewmembers to return to the ship briefly at 10:00 a.m. "to prevent looting or attempts to salvage by unauthorized personnel."

It has long been rumored that the crew spent many months in Scituate, socializing with the local citizens, especially the young women intrigued by these young Italian men. According to Giovanni, nothing could be further from the truth. In fact, most of the crew was placed on a bus by midday of the seventeenth and brought to Boston. Giovanni said, "After we were transferred to the Seaman's Friend's Society in Boston, we stayed about fifteen days with the hope to refloat the ship. It was not possible due to more rough seas and because the ship was high on the beach. We then flew home

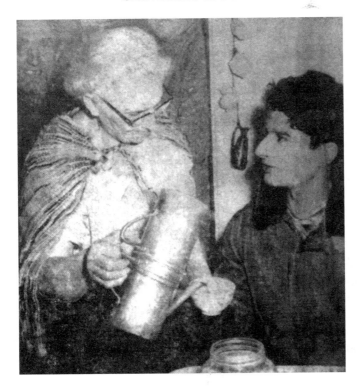

Lina Russo serving coffee to nineteen-year-old Giovanni Belfiore during the rescue. Lina was from Italy but from a different village than the crew. She opened up her home to the crew and rescuers, serving food and translating.

to Italy." Captain Traini and several officers stayed behind to help with the salvage of the *Etrusco*. One week after the rescue, the Coast Guard presented Lina Russo with a plaque which read: "First Coast Guard District Award of Appreciation to Mrs. Lina Russo through whose thoughtful kindness food and shelter were provided coastguardsmen during the rescue of the SS Etrusco at Scituate, Mass. March 17 1956."

The *Etrusco*'s grounding alongside Scituate Light—"parallel parked," as many said—caused a sensation. Each weekend through the next six months, thousands of people, even up to fifty thousand by one estimate, weaved their cars through Scituate to Cedar Point to view the ship. Local businesses were hampered, town resources were strained cleaning up and managing the masses and local residents were becoming increasingly alarmed that the ship would be cut up and scrapped. Removing this debris from the small road around Scituate would have done extensive damage. L'Italica Di Navigazione, owners of the *Etrusco*, gave up any hope of removing the ship and settled with their insurers, who in turn sold the vessel to Victor Transport for $121,211, or one tenth of its previous value. Victor Transport had plans

Lebbeus Curtus, who salvaged and cleared Pearl Harbor in 1942, was now in charge of getting the *Etrusco* off the beach. *Courtesy Scituate Historical Society.*

to remove the *Etrusco* from the beach and put it back in service. To pull this off, it turned to Lebbeus Curtus, the seventy-five-year-old former chief of salvage for the United States during World War II. He was credited with successfully salvaging 230 vessels at Pearl Harbor and Okinawa. Of note, the *Etrusco* grounded in the same spot where the ship *Elizabeth*, captained by a relative of Lebbeus Curtus, grounded ninety-seven years earlier.

Curtus's plan was simple: patch the holes in the ship with cement, weld plates over the larger holes and pump water out of the vessel. Next, he placed three large compressors on the deck to power the winches and set five eight-ton anchors one thousand feet offshore rigged to a block and tackle system. Then, he would use the ship's winches to pull the block and tackle, turning the ship from parallel to ninety degrees off shore and pull it to deeper water. Work on this plan started in September and was estimated to take two months. With the rig in place, actual pulling began in late September one hour before and after each high tide. By October 5, the ship had been turned ninety degrees. After dynamiting several large rocks out of the way and digging a channel, the path was becoming clear for the ship's

Crowds, as many as fifty thousand people in one day, rushed to Scituate each weekend from March to November 1956 to view the beached vessel. *Courtesty Scituate Historical Society.*

complete removal. Curtus planned to flood the bow, which was now floating at high tide, which would then lift the stern off the shore, and pull! Several years ago, I flew a small plane over where the *Etrusco* beached, and you can still make out the channel where she was dragged off extending about one hundred yards into the water, with rocks depressed and seaweed not yet quite fully grown back.

As the imminent removal of the ship became obvious, media attention and the number of sightseers soared. Over fifty thousand people showed up on Columbus Day, the predicted day to drag the ship off the shore. On this particular day, they were disappointed; however, by late November, all conditions were favorable and finally on Thanksgiving, November 22, a nearly eleven-foot tide and offshore winds proved optimal. Shortly after 2:00 p.m., the *Etrusco* and Cedar Point parted company. Tugs from Boston arrived an hour later to escort the ship to Boston. She arrived at the Bethlehem Shipyard in East Boston eight hours later and eight months after that fateful

The *Etrusco* was turned ninety degrees, pulled out to sea during high tide and towed to a shipyard in East Boston for repairs on November 22, 1956. *Courtesy Scituate Historical Society.*

night in March. The hull was surveyed and reinforcing plates were installed on the bottom. After being overhauled, the *Etrusco* was renamed the *Scituate* and rechristened by Anne Tilden, from one of the oldest and most prominent families in Scituate, on December 20, 1956. It operated as the *Scituate* for eight more years, eventually being scrapped in 1964 in Hong Kong.

Although in town for less than a day, Giovanni Belfiore had fond memories of the beauty of Scituate and its friendly people, especially Lina Russo. After leaving Scituate, he remarkably saw the *Etrusco* again:

> *After Etrusco, I joined Villain and Fassio, an Italian shipping company, and we made regular voyages between Italy and the US calling at New York, Baltimore, Philadelphia, Norfolk and Charleston. During one of*

Giovanni Belfiore in 2005. Though not in Scituate long, he has fond memories of the rescuers and locals, particularly Lina Russo.

these voyages around 1959 or 1960, when I was on the bridge, I was second officer; I met a Fort type vessel. We passed close and when I saw her name was Scituate on the bow, I said to myself that was very strange to meet a ship with this name. Then I went to see the Lloyd's List and I found out that after this ship's name Scituate was written ex Etrusco. I realize the ship was refloated.

Giovanni went back to sea after the *Etrusco* grounding, serving on many cargo vessels around the world. He passed away in 2010, five years after I met him in Genoa.

CHAPTER 2

CITY OF SALISBURY

OFF GRAVES LIGHT

42° 22.39 N
70° 51.56 W

A s the *Etrusco* headed north to the yards of East Boston, on her port side, she would have sailed by and over many wrecks and the navigational aids set in place to prevent them, just as you would today. Her route is marked by three prominent lighthouses, which guard dangerous ledges off Cohasset and Boston that have claimed many ships and lives. Probably the most interesting is the wreck of the *City of Salisbury*, which sank near Graves Light in 1938 with a cargo of exotic animals, earning the nickname "The Zoo Wreck." Before discussing that wreck however, we should spend some time on these lighthouses: Minot's, Boston and Graves.

Off the shore of Cohasset, five miles north of where the *Etrusco* grounded, lays a large pile of dangerous rocks slightly covered by the choppy waters and half tide. This area known as Minot's Ledge, where Minot's Lighthouse now sits, has been infamous for centuries as one of New England's most dangerous areas. The Quonahassit Indian tribe, from which Cohasset derived its name, believed the ledge was doomed. They would visit the rocks and leave gifts to please the spirit they believed haunted the rocks. It was believed that if the spirit were to become angry, it would create devastating storms that would completely wipe out or destroy the Indian communities. We know of over forty shipwrecks that occurred in just twenty years (before the lighthouse was built), causing severe damage to property and loss of life; many more unrecorded wrecks undoubtedly have happened on the ledge. It is fortunate that the *Etrusco*, as she drifted toward Scituate Light, did not hit the ledge, as it would have been extremely difficult to save the crew as they had been in Scituate.

Building a lighthouse was a widely accepted as a necessity among the mariners of Mass Bay. In March 1847, Congress finally appropriated $20,000 for a lighthouse on the ledge; an additional $19,500 would eventually be needed for the completion of the project, including $4,500 for the lighting apparatus. Built as a nine iron "erector set" piled into the rocks, the lighthouse was finished in late 1849. It was lighted for the first time on January 1, 1850, but not before tragedy struck one more time, to a ship filled with Irish immigrants.

The mid-nineteenth century brought a huge influx of immigrants to large U.S. ports like Boston and New York. This was due, in part, to the end of the Napoleonic War, which made it safer to travel on the oceans. One of the countries to heavily emigrate was Ireland. By the 1840s, the potato blight was in full swing, causing widespread starvation across the entire country. This forced many poor and starving Irish citizens to leave their homelands in hope of a better life. Many ships made it safely to America, but some, such as the *St. John*, were not as fortunate and became coffin ships.

The immigrant ship *St. John*, with over 140 Irish immigrants aboard, sailed from Galway, Ireland, to Boston on September 5, 1849. All seemed to be going well until early October, when a large storm hit as it entered Mass Bay. Hours into the storm, Captain Oliver and the crew were able to identify the *Kathleen*, a British brig that was anchored off Cohasset. Hoping to gain the protection of a landlocked harbor, Oliver ran before the wind, dropping anchor inside Minot's ledge and the newly completed but unlighted Minot's Ledge Lighthouse. The crew was ordered to cut down the masts in an attempt to dampen the effects of the tumultuous weather. Much to the crew's dismay, the storm proved to be too strong and ominously swept the ship onto a large ledge called Grampus Rocks, taking the lives of most of the immigrants aboard.

Preferring not, as tradition demanded, to go down with his ship, the captain and eleven passengers made it onto a longboat and were luckily rescued. Although these lucky twelve were saved, the rescue boat assumed they were the only passengers alive and instead of returning to the wreck to save others, moved on to the *Kathleen*, leaving the immigrants stranded in the violent water and on the ship. Three stories of individuals highlight this tragedy. The first involved an Irish man named Patrick Sweeney who boarded the ship along with his wife and nine children. When the ship wrecked, Sweeney held his youngest child to his chest and tried to swim toward land. Tragically, the intensity of the waves overpowered him, drowning them both, along with the rest of his family. In one fell sweep of nature, an entire family was wiped out. The second story was of a young Irishman who decided to accompany his sisters to America on the *St. John*. When the wreck occurred, he jumped into the water and was soon rescued by a boat. Upon arriving on shore, the young boy learned that both his sisters had died in the wreck. Finally, the last story is of a young mother who had landed in America months earlier. She awaited a woman who was transporting her youngest child to her on the *St. John*. When the wreck occurred, she walked down to the scene to search for the pair and, upon opening a coffin, found the woman dead, still holding the dead child in her arms.

This event was so dramatic that it inspired author Henry David Thoreau to visit Cohasset two days after reading about the wreck in the newspaper. He rushed to the scene, as psychologist Carl Jung could have predicted, because he found "the disaster titillating, a weird physiological arousal, and an animal stimulation" and wrote one of his most tragic and gruesome stories. His recollections were published a few years later under the title *The Shipwreck* in June 1855. Thoreau always wrote with precise detail and, as a transcendentalist, looked at each of his subjects with extreme interest. Here is how Thoreau put it:

Hopeful Irish Almost Reached United States

By Tom Noonan
(United Press Staff Correspondent)

Cohasset, Mass., Oct. 8 (UP)—A violent nor'easter raged 100 years ago Friday along the New England coast studded with death traps of jagged rocks.

Somewhere offshore the brig Saint John labored in mountainous seas as it neared the end of a stormy voyage with a band of Irish emigrants.

Land was sighted amid driving rain and murk when dawn broke. But already the hopes of emigrants from famine-ridden Ireland for a fresh start in a new world had given way to fears for their very lives.

Almost none of the emigrants ever reached America alive. For within a few horror-filled hours the Saint John became the most disastrous shipwreck ever to occur in the outer reaches of Boston harbor.

Only 12 Live

One hundred and forty-three persons perished in the boiling waters near Minot's Light including 99 emigrants. Only 12 survived including Captain Oliver, skipper of the brig, and a 14-year-old Irish lad who was a stowaway.

Newspaper report on the devastating Irish immigrant shipwreck *St. John*.

The brig St. John, from Galway, Ireland, laden with emigrants, was wrecked on Sunday morning; it was now Tuesday morning, and the sea was still breaking violently on the rocks. There were eighteen or twenty of the same large boxes that I have mentioned, lying on a green hill-side, a few rods from the water, and surrounded by a crowd. The bodies which had been recovered, twenty-seven or eight in all, had been collected there…I witnessed no signs of grief, but there was a sober despatch of business which was affecting…I saw many marble feet and matted heads as the cloths were raised, and one livid, swollen, and mangled body of a drowned girl—who probably had intended to go out to service in some American family—to which some rags still adhered, with a string, half concealed by the flesh, about its swollen neck; the coiled-up wreck of a human hulk, gashed by the rocks or fishes, so that the bone and muscle were exposed, but quite bloodless—merely red and white—with wide-open and staring eyes, yet lustreless, dead-lights; or like the cabin windows of a stranded vessel, filled with sand. Sometimes there were two or more children, or a parent and child, in the same box, and on the lid would perhaps be written with red chalk, "Bridget such-a-one, and sister's child."

Minister Joseph Osgood conducted a funeral service for the one hundred or so victims who washed up on the beach or were recovered from the wreck. Forty-five bodies were laid to rest in a grave at a Cohasset cemetery; a second funeral was held for the Irish victims, this one being Catholic while the first one Unitarian. The large Celtic stone cross that marks the graves of the victims of the *St. John* is still remembered each year. People from Cohasset and Ireland and descendants from the shipwreck come to remember the lives lost. We will see in our last chapter on the *Forest Queen* that not all wrecks end in the loss of life. The *Forest Queen* washed ashore off Scituate in 1953, with all forty-five Irish immigrants reaching shore safely and moving on to a better life.

Shortly after the wreck of the *St. John* and fourteen months after Minot's Light was lighted, tragedy struck again. On April 16, 1851, a deadly storm hit Minot's Ledge causing the light to crumble and taking the lives of two innocent young men, Joseph Wilson and Joseph Antoine. The two young men were temporarily looking after the lighthouse while the permanent keeper was ashore. They enclosed a letter in a bottle and threw it out into the sea as they accepted the harsh reality of the storm. Picked up the next day by a Gloucester fisherman, their note read, "The lighthouse won't stand over to night. She shakes 2 feet each way now. J.W. + J.A." There had been several lighthouse keepers who thought the original Minot's Ledge Lighthouse was unstable and dangerous. One of the final complaints made before the structure was torn into the water was by John W. Bennett. He wrote that

Iron Lighthouse on Minot's Rock, published in the *New Yorker* in 1849. Constructed beginning in 1847 by driving nine iron piles into the ledge, this first Minot's Light was wrecked on April 16, 1851, only fourteen months after it was lighted.

"the rods put into the lower section are bent up in fantastic shapes; some are torn asunder from their fastenings; the ice is so massive that there is no appearance of the ladder...the northern part of the foundation is split and the light house shakes at least two feet each way." The community shared the same question: Why would one build a nine-iron pile lighthouse so unlike all other lighthouses?

Reconstruction of a second Minot's Light began in 1855 and was completed in 1860, this time using a traditional solid granite cylinder 110 feet high. The work was not easy or safe; when a wave hit, the men learned to hold on tightly to a steel bolt or a rope until the danger passed. Only workers who could swim were allowed to work on the project. The new Minot's Light was designed by General Joseph G. Totten of the Lighthouse Board, and it has been called the greatest achievement in American lighthouse engineering. There are several legends tied to Minot's Light. After the quick downfall of

Drawing by A.R. Waud of the second Minot's Light, completed in 1860, which appeared in *Harper's Weekly* on July 10, 1869.

the first structure, it was recorded that there were many "ghostly" presences around and inside the lighthouse. One of the most bizarre legends is that of the "clean windows." Seagulls flying overhead dirty the windows; cleaning them usually takes the whole day. If a keeper mentioned to his assistant that they needed cleaning, by the time the assistant would make it up with cleaning implements, the windows would be sparkling clean again. Minot's Light is also known as "Lover's Ledge" due to the light pattern "1-4-3," which is a common way to symbolize "I Love You." In 1956, as we do still today, the crew of the *Etrusco* would have seen Minot's Light flashing this sentimental greeting as it passed by.

Lighthouses and legends seem to go together, and Boston Light is no exception. Built in 1716 on Little Brewster Island marking the southern entrance to Boston Harbor, Boston Light is the nation's oldest standing lighthouse. Its first keeper, George Worthylake, along with his wife and daughter, capsized on a boat trip to the mainland. It is believed that they haunt the structure, with equipment going on and off by itself, a little girl's laugh and the silhouette of a woman all being reported. During the Revolutionary War, as the British controlled the harbor, Boston Light was attacked and

Boston Light, originally built in 1716, is the oldest lighthouse in the United States.

burned on two occasions by American forces. As the British forces withdrew in 1776, they blew up the tower and completely destroyed it. The lighthouse was eventually reconstructed in 1783, to the same seventy-five-foot height as the original tower. In 1856, it was raised to its present height of ninety-eight feet and a new lantern room added. Boston Light became the last lighthouse to be fully automated and now operates twenty-four hours a day.

Close by Boston Light on Castle Island, Edgar Allan Poe learned of a gruesome murder while serving there in the army; it became the inspiration for his story "The Cask of Amontillado." Perhaps the most tragic of the spirits wandering near Boston Light is the so-called Woman in Black. Trying to free her husband from the Civil War prison at Fort Warren on George's Island, Melanie Lanier was captured and hung wearing a black dress. Just to the north of Boston Light is the Graves, an aggregation of rock outcroppings. The Graves is not named after the many ships that went to their graves around these dangerous rocks, as one would think, but named after Thomas Graves, a prominent trader in the colonial period and resident of Lynn. There is some dispute, however, that it may be named after the Thomas Graves who was a seventeenth-century British admiral.

The Graves is the location of Graves Light, the tallest lighthouse in Boston Harbor at 113 feet. At the outermost rocks of the harbor, Graves Light is an important navigation aid for traffic to and from the port, particularly from the northern reaches of Mass Bay. It was built in 1905 at the same time the North Channel into Boston Harbor was dredged to become the principal entrance for large vessels. It is a conical design using granite blocks on a granite foundation. The light was the setting for the climactic storm in the 1948 film *Portrait of Jennie*. Prior to that film, it was the scene of three famous wrecks.

In 1936, the *Romance* sank after a collision with the steamer *New York* during heavy fog, with all aboard safely rescued. In the early morning of January 21, 1941, the fishing schooner *Mary E. O'Hara* passed Graves Light and headed for the inner harbor. According to Edward Rowe Snow, suddenly there was a crash as the ship struck an anchored barge and the *O'Hara* slowly sank in forty feet of water. The frightened men scrambled up into the rigging and waited to be rescued. One by one, they dropped off as their strength failed. When rescuers came at dawn only five of the twenty-four crewmembers remained. The loss of nineteen men made it one of the worst disasters in the history of Boston Harbor but not the strangest. For that, we turn to the *City of Salisbury*.

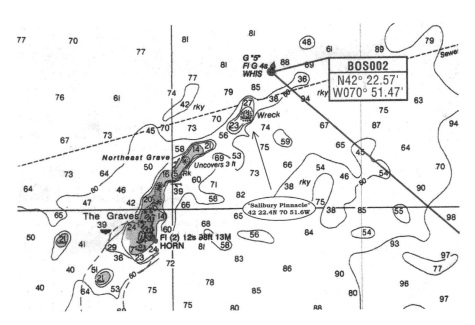

Nautical chart showing Graves Light and pinnacle where the *City of Salisbury* wrecked in 1938. Similar to the chart used in 1938, this chart, NOAA number 13270, has been updated many times, most recently July 14, 2001.

City of Salisbury

The steel-hulled British freighter *City of Salisbury* was built in Sunderland, England, in 1924 by the Wear Shipyard of W. Gray & Co., Ltd. She was 419 feet long, had a 54-foot beam and displaced 6,000 tons. The master was Captain Oscar Harris, who hailed from Liverpool, England. Bound for New York with a cargo estimated at nearly $2 million, the steamer was nearing completion of a ten-thousand-mile odyssey, which included stops in Calcutta, India, Ceylon, the Malay States, Halifax, Nova Scotia and now Boston. The animal cargo made for an interesting voyage. Before leaving Calcutta, a Himalayan bear had escaped. Later at sea a king cobra cannibalized its mate, and at Halifax, twenty-five monkeys escaped.

The weather was clear on Saturday, April 23, 1938, as Boston pilot Captain William H. Lewis guided the *City of Salisbury* toward the outer harbor en route to New York. Lewis was positive of his position, with government charts showing thirty-three feet of water northeast of Graves Ledge Light, over which the steamer should have easily passed. But without warning, the weather turned and engulfed the *City of Salisbury* in a heavy fog. Soon thereafter, the ship hit a seemingly uncharted pinnacle reef projecting to within twenty-two feet of the surface at mean low tide and drove hard aground. The pinnacle, over which the bow and stern hung, supported the ship's midsection. As ships have more strength when completely supported by water, the ebb and flow of the tide combined with a ground swell put undue stresses on the hull. Shortly after the freighter grounded, she broke in two, and all but a skeleton crew of fourteen men and four officers were removed off the stern by a tug. The next day, strange noises were heard

Illustration of *City of Salisbury* on top of the pinnacle on the day of wreck. *Michelle Garcia, illustrator.*

emanating from deep within the steamer's hull. Not long after noon, the vessel began to strain and heave. The *New York Times* reported: "As officers and men hurried to the afterdeck there was a crash from within the vessel, the forward portion rolled to starboard and, amid a swirl of the otherwise calm waters, disappeared from sight. The *City of Salisbury* had broken just forward of the stack."

By midsummer, the forward section had slipped into deep water and what remained on the pinnacle was showing signs of stress. A crack had developed mid length of the half ship. About two weeks before the stern broke up, author Edward Rowe Snow visited the wreck and wrote, "It was a weird sensation…the grinding and gnashing of the iron rods and broken timbers far down under the water could plainly be heard, and the steamer would shudder and jerk as the ground swell passed alongside." For most of the year, excursion boats visited the wreck, making it one of the most spectacular and widely viewed shipping disasters in Mass Bay, a title it held until the grounding of the *Etrusco* eighteen years later. Late that fall, according to Rowe, after surviving the Great Hurricane of September 21,

City of Salisbury on top of the pinnacle, broken in two, several days after the wreck. Note Graves Light in the background. *Courtesy William Quinn.*

1938, the vessel rolled off the ledge during an October nor'easter and now rests in twenty to ninety feet of water.

According to Henry Keats in his book *New England's Legacy of Shipwrecks*, the cargo was worth three times the value of the steamer, making it the most expensive wreck in Boston Harbor. Most of the *City of Salisbury*'s cargo of exotic animals, including forty pythons, forty cobras, three hundred monkeys and twenty crates of rare birds, was removed prior to the vessel breaking in two. Shortly after the bow settled away, its cargo began to float out of the hold. Prevailing currents carried it toward Nantasket Beach and the South Shore. In addition to rubber and bales of jute, large wicker containers held various species of birds, monkeys, pythons, deadly cobras and other exotic animals. According to news reports, some monkeys escaped during the disaster and climbed up the rigging. One large, badly decomposed snake washed ashore on Race Point Beach and was mistaken for a sea serpent by locals.

By August, a salvage crew from New York had removed much of what was in the after section of the ship. According to Snow, as late as 1963, divers were still removing cargo from her broken holds. Over the years, her hull was extensively blasted and much of the steel removed for scrap. An investigation by the Coast Guard cleared Captain Lewis of any wrongdoing after finding

Illustration of exotic zoo animals, such as monkeys and snakes, escaping the wreck. *Michelle Garcia, illustrator.*

Drowned animals and debris washed onshore all over Mass Bay. Here we see a large python, initially thought to be a sea monster, washed up on Race Point, Provincetown.

that Government Chart #246 incorrectly marked the depth of the pinnacle, which is now known as Salisbury Pinnacle. A popular diving spot that I visited in 2010, the wreck now consists of broken and scattered steel plates. In 1995, Michael Miller and three other local divers brought up the thirteen-foot, six-thousand-pound anchor, encrusted with scale and barnacles, from the British freighter.

This incident, as well as the *Etrusco* grounding, points to two factors that play a key role in shipwrecks: the severity of the weather and quality of the aids to navigation. Let's take a brief look at the development of marine navigation and weather forecasting to try to answer this question: how could a modern freighter with an experienced Boston Harbor pilot hit a rock in the channel and sink?

Many locations in the United States have the saying that if you don't like the weather, wait a minute, and this is true in Mass Bay. New England weather is arguably among the most varied in the world. It includes both hot and cold temperatures, droughts, heavy rainfall, hurricanes, tornadoes, blizzards and more. Mark Twain captured the richness of New England weather, saying in 1935: "Now as to the size of the weather in New England—lengthways, I mean. It is utterly disproportionate to the size of that little country. Half the time, when it is packed as full as it can stick, you will see New England weather sticking out beyond the edges and projecting around hundreds and hundreds of miles over the neighboring States. She can't hold a tenth part of her weather."

Four important components dominate New England weather. First, located between the equator and the North Pole, it is a battleground for warm, moist air from the south and cold, dry air from the north. Warm, cold and stationary fronts frequently traverse the region, bringing one air mass to another in rapid succession. Second, the region is dominated by cold water from the Labrador Current along its northeast coast and the warm water Gulf Stream along the southeast. Sea breezes are generated by the temperature difference between the cooler water and warmer land. In winter, coastal waters remain warm relative to land areas making it difficult for forecasters to predict snow-rain boundaries. Third, since New England falls primarily in the westerlies, the area is dominated by drier air from across North America, rather than a prevailing wind from off the Atlantic Ocean. Fourth, New England's many mountains enhance precipitation on the windward side and create drier conditions known as the "rain shadow" effect on the downwind slopes.

As noted, the prevailing winds across most of New England are westerly. However, winds can, and do, come from all directions on the compass. North and northwest winds deliver cold and dry air from Canada; westerly winds bring upper-Midwest air to the region, warmed slightly when passing over the Great Lakes. Southwesterly winds are common in New England, especially in Mass Bay, particularly after the passage of a warm front, which can carry warm and humid air from the Gulf of Mexico and Caribbean. South and southeast winds are hot or warm and humid, though less frequent. East and northeast winds are cool and humid, as the air takes in the cooler water of the Labrador Current and northern Atlantic Ocean. Northeast winds in New England are frequently associated with coastal nor'easters.

A nor'easter is a type of coastal storm so-called because it travels up the coast from the south and the winds come from the northeast. The sharp contrast between the cold Labrador Current and the warm Gulf Stream make these storms dangerous and frequent. Nor'easters can cause severe coastal flooding and erosion, hurricane force winds and heavy snow or rain depending on when the storm occurs. Nor'easters can occur at any time of the year but are known mostly as winter storms. The most devastating nor'easters in Mass Bay were the *Portland* Gale of 1898, the Perfect Storm of 1991, which we will discuss later, and the Blizzard of '78. I was living on Second Cliff in Scituate during this storm and was an eyewitness to the destruction. The Blizzard of '78 formed on February 5, 1978, and broke up on February 7, 1978. Dumping a record twenty-seven-plus inches of snow in the Boston area, it killed approximately 100 people, 2 sadly on Scituate's

Cedar Point near where the *Etrusco* grounded, and injured around 4,500. It also caused over $520 million in damage.

Interestingly, the term "nor'easter" is a combination of "nore," meaning north, in association with the points of the compass and wind direction. There is evidence the "noreast" was used as early as 1594; the first recorded use of the term nor'easter occurred in 1836 in a translation of Aristophanes. The term nor'easter naturally developed from the historical spellings and pronunciations of the compass points and the direction of wind or sailing, though some linguists claim it was non-sailors—"landlubbers" such as poets, writers and journalists—that developed this usage, as mariners most likely would have referred to north-northeast as "no'nuth'east." Regardless of its origin, the term nor'easter is now widely used to describe a coastal storm.

In the last four centuries, there have been many hurricanes that have struck New England with brute force, leveling forests of trees, battering the shores with huge waves, flooding towns and rivers in quick fashion and sinking ships at sea. Three hurricanes have made a lasting impression on historians. One was known as the Great Colonial Hurricane of 1635. The eye of the storm evidently passed between Plymouth and Boston, and winds were estimated at 140 miles per hour, a deadly Category Four hurricane. It would be 180 years later that a storm of equal strength occurred with the so-called Great September Gale of 1815. As the *City of Salisbury* hung on the pinnacle rock six months after grounding, a hurricane dubbed the Great Hurricane formed in September 1938 and slowly evolved into one of the worst hurricanes ever, killing over 708 people and damaging twenty-five thousand homes.

Ancient weather forecasting methods usually relied on observed patterns of events, experience and local knowledge. For example, New England fishermen may have observed that if the sunset was particularly red, the following day often brought fair weather. To help remember this, we have the famous and true saying "red at night, sailors delight; red in morning, sailors take warning." The first major aid to weather forecasting was the barometer, a scientific instrument invented in Italy in the 1640s and used to measure atmospheric pressure. It was not, however, until the invention of the electric telegraph in 1835 that the modern age of weather forecasting began. The telegraph allowed reports of weather conditions from a wide area to be received almost instantaneously, enabling forecasts to be made from knowledge of weather conditions further upwind. The two men most credited with the birth of forecasting as a science were Francis Beaufort, remembered chiefly for the Beaufort scale, which rated wind and waves, and

Robert Fitzroy, developer of the improved Fitzroy barometer. At the turn of the nineteenth century, radio communications were now possible from great distances on land and over water to ships, and by 1925, public radio forecasts were being made by Boston stations. Forecasters have made great strides in the last six decades spurred by the development of programmable electronic computers.

In 1938, the pilot aboard the *City of Salisbury* would have had excellent local knowledge of weather patterns and sea conditions and a marine radio. Despite these advantages, he still succumbed to a fast-moving fog bank. Created by warm moist air moving over cold water, fog is a frequent contributor to shipwrecks along Mass Bay. Especially when winds blow from the east and southeast over the Gulf Stream, they are loaded with warm moisture. Combine that wind with the cold Arctic water around Newfoundland and Nova Scotia, brought in to the area by the Labrador Current, and the conditions are ripe for fog. As the air cools, it can no longer hold as much moisture, and condensation creates tiny water droplets. Called advection fog, this creates a dangerous situation for many mariners, especially prior to the development of radar. It can form quickly with little warning, as the pilot of the *City of Salisbury* discovered and as we will learn later, as did the captains of the *Fairfax* and *Pinthis*. To prevent collisions with other ships, bells and whistles are sounded loudly and frequently. We will also see, with the *Portland* Gale in 1898, the wreck of the *Chester A. Poling* in 1977 and the Perfect Storm in 1991, that weather forecasting is still an inaccurate science, though vastly improved.

To prevent collisions with rocks and the shore, mariners rely on proper navigation aids such as Minot's, Boston and Graves lighthouses discussed above. They also rely on charts, compasses and a myriad of other equipment. In 1938, the pilot aboard the *City of Salisbury* would have had the best government charts available at the time, a compass, radio and years of experience piloting around Boston Harbor, and still he succumbed to an inaccurate chart. A more prudent pilot would have kept this mariner's rule in mind: never rely solely on any single aid to navigation, particularly on floating aids.

Around four thousand years ago, the Phoenicians were the first western civilization that used navigation at sea. Phoenician sailors navigated by using primitive charts and observations of the sun and stars to determine location. In the Northern Hemisphere, mariners could determine latitude easily by measuring the altitude of the North Star above the horizon. The angle in degrees was the latitude of the ship. One of the earliest man-made navigational tools was the mariner's compass, which was an early form of the magnetic compass. Until the fifteenth century, however, mariners were essentially coastal navigators. Sailing on the open sea was limited to regions of predictable winds and currents or where there was a wide continental shelf to follow.

Around 1730, English mathematician John Hadley and American inventor Thomas Godfrey separately invented the sextant, at the same time but an ocean apart. The sextant provided mariners with a more accurate means of determining the angle between the horizon and the sun, moon or stars in order to calculate latitude. During the sixteenth century, the chip log was invented and used as a crude speedometer. A line containing knots at regular intervals and weighted to drag in the water was let out over the stern as the ship was underway. A seaman would count the number of knots that went out over a specific period of time, and the ship's speed could then be calculated.

While latitude could be found relatively accurately using celestial navigation, longitude could only be estimated. This was because the measurement of longitude is made by comparing the difference in time between the mariner's starting location and new location. Even some of the best clocks of the early eighteenth century could lose as much as ten minutes per day, which translated into a computational error of 150 miles or more. In 1764, British clockmaker John Harrison invented the seagoing chronometer, the most important advance to marine navigation in the three millennia. In 1779, British naval officer and explorer Captain James Cook used Harrison's chronometer to circumnavigate the globe. When he returned, his calculations of longitude based on the chronometer proved correct to within 8 miles. From information he gathered on his voyage, Cook completed many detailed charts of the world that completely changed the nature of navigation. In 1884, by international agreement, the Prime Meridian located at 0° longitude was established as the meridian passing through Greenwich, England.

During the mid-thirteenth century, mariners began recording detailed records of their voyages on charts. These first charts were not very accurate but were considered valuable and often kept secret from other mariners. There was no latitude or longitude labeled on them, but between major ports there was a compass rose indicating the direction to travel. The term "compass rose" comes from the figure's compass points, which resemble rose petals. A modern nautical chart depicts the nature and shape of the coast, water depths and general topography of the ocean floor, locations of navigational danger, the rise and fall of tides and locations of human made aids to navigation. It is one of the most fundamental tools available to mariners, who use charts to plan voyages and navigate ships using the shortest, safest and most economical routes. Since its inception in 1807, NOAA's Office of Coast Survey, or just Coast Survey, has produced accurate nautical charts to support maritime commerce and promote safety at sea.

According to NOAA, in early nineteenth-century America, when the new Coast Survey began its work, shipping between the states was mostly on water as shipping goods on land was too difficult. Foreign trade, correspondence, travel to Europe and, of course, commercial fishing was conducted at sea. Despite the importance of marine navigation, few charts were available to safely guide mariners in their pursuits; the charts that were available were old. By 1835, hydrographic surveys using lead lines to measure the depth and bottom configuration of water bodies were being conducted, notably in New York Harbor. Along with soundings, these reports included descriptions of local trade and commerce, fishing practices, port facilities and shipwrecks and offer a wealth of information to historians. Data displayed on today's charts is collected by multibeam and side-scan sonar, which provide a comprehensive sweep of the sea bottom. A nautical chart today might carry data from multiple eras and comes in electronic and paper formats.

The twentieth century brought important advances in other areas of marine navigation. The gyro compass was introduced in 1907; its primary benefit over a magnetic compass is that the gyro is unaffected by the Earth's, or the ship's, magnetic field and always points to true north. The first practical radar system was produced in 1935. It was used to locate objects beyond range of vision by projecting radio waves against them. This was, and still is, very useful on ships to locate other ships and land when visibility is reduced. The navigation system known as Long Range Navigation—LORAN—was developed between 1940 and 1943 and uses pulsed radio transmissions to determine a ship's position. In the late twentieth century, GPS largely replaced the LORAN. GPS uses the same principle of time difference from separate signals as LORAN, but the signals come from satellites. Most oceangoing vessels keep a sextant onboard only in case of an emergency. When I was navigator in the U.S. Navy in the 1980s, we had to "shoot stars" each morning, that is, use a sextant to determine angles of stars and plot a fix; this skill is no longer practiced on board.

CHAPTER 3

CHESTER A. POLING

GLOUCESTER

42° 34.25 N
70° 40.15W

As we have seen, many factors play a role in a ship wrecking, such as the weather, aids to navigation and design. We have discussed the dynamic nature of New England weather, especially nor'easters and fog; the importance of accurate charts and navigations aids such as lighthouses; and how an underpowered ship such as the *Etrusco* is at the mercy of powerful storms. We have also seen that despite technological advances with all these factors, shipwrecks continue to occur. A recent example is the Italian cruise ship *Costa Concordia*, which was carrying 4,200 passengers and crew when it struck a reef off the Tuscan island of Giglio on January 13, 2012, in daylight and fine weather. She took on water and started listing badly; thirty people perished. Closer to home in Gloucester, we have the *Chester A. Poling*.

Gloucester was founded at Cape Ann by an expedition called the Dorchester Company from Dorchester, England, chartered by James I in 1623. It was one of the first English settlements in what would become the Massachusetts Bay Colony. Life in this first settlement was harsh and short and, around 1626, abandoned. The settlers moved to Naumkeag (what is now called Salem), where more fertile soil for planting was found. The town was formally incorporated in 1642 and took the name Gloucester from the city of Gloucester in southwest England. It became an important shipbuilding center; the first schooner was reputedly built there in 1713 and "schooned" or skipped across the harbor when launched.

The community developed into an important fishing port, largely due to its proximity to Georges Bank and other fishing banks off the east coast of Nova Scotia and Newfoundland. Seafaring and fishing have been, and still are, very dangerous; in its over 370-year history, Gloucester has lost an estimated ten thousand mariners. The names of those lost are painted on a huge mural in the main staircase at city hall, and of course, "they that go down to the sea in ships" are honored in the famous monument showing a helmsman looking to the sea. Fisheries have historically been treated as common property, which according to researchers can lead to overfishing. A different

They That Go Down to the Sea in Ships. Gloucester, Massachusetts.

method of managing these grounds involves what is called catch shares. Catch shares remove the common property nature of the fishery by providing security, exclusivity and, in some cases, tradability to the resource through individual quotas, cooperatives or area-based harvest rights.

Today, as with the Navigation Acts of 1651, controversy continues to build regarding the regulation of this important resource. On one side, we have NOAA and other proponents of catch share who claim it will ensure that fisheries are sustainable pitted against Mass Bay fishermen who claim it is misguided, overly dramatic and self-serving regulation. Gloucester fishermen, supported by excellent investigative reporting by the *Gloucester Times*, have led on this issue. This dilemma is highlighted in a 2012 National Geographic network series called "Wicked Tuna," which promotes the show as follows: "Fishing is a hard life, and harder with bluefin stocks depleted. In Gloucester, Massachusetts, there's a special breed of fishermen. For generations they've used rod and reel to catch

Chester A Poling underway, circa 1975.

the elusive bluefin tuna. They depend on these fish for their livelihood, and the competition is brutal."

The *Chester A. Poling* was a steel coastal tanker that carried kerosene heating oil. It was originally built by United Drydocks, Inc., at Mariners Harbor, Staten Island, New York, in 1934 and named the *Plattsburg Sacony*. In 1956, the Avondale Shipyard added 29.3 additional feet to make her 282 feet overall, with a beam of 40 and a depth of 17 feet. Her gross tonnage was 1,546, and she was propelled by two General Motors twelve-cylinder oil engines. In 1962, she was renamed the *Mobile Albany*; the Poling Transportation Company of New York City then bought and renamed her *Chester A. Poling* in 1969. According to Massachusetts Coastal Zone Management, at 6:30 a.m. on January 10, 1977, the coastal tanker left Everett, Massachusetts, bound for Newington, New Hampshire. As she passed Graves Light and the wreck of the *City of Salisbury*, she was in ballast, that is, without cargo, having unloaded her kerosene from Bayway, New Jersey.

Captain Charles Burgess knew it would be a rough passage as the National Weather Service forecasted thirty-five mile per hour winds with seas fifteen to twenty feet. Although his ship was forty-three years old, Burgess was confident the tanker was in good working condition, having passed its annual Coast Guard inspection each year without incident. However, by late morning, the weather had worsened. Winds neared fifty miles per hour, and seas were thirty feet in height. Waves pummeled the vessels starboard bow, tossing the craft about. To give his ship greater stability in the worsening conditions, Captain Burgess flooded four of the ship's six cargo tanks with seawater. Just before 10:30 a.m., within minutes of a course change that would have

Depiction of a wave crashing over the *Chester A. Poling* on January 10, 1977. *Michelle Garcia, illustrator.*

put the vessel on a northwesterly heading to better meet the seas, a huge wave smashed the tanker, breaking it in two, twenty-seven feet forward of amidships. "We were hit by a wave, one of those big waves maybe thirty feet high," said crewman Harry Selleck of Pawtucket, Rhode Island, who was on the bridge with Captain Burgess. "It just came in and broke the ship in half… she caught the ship just the right way." The force of the storm subsequently bent the bow backward until it was parallel with the stern.

Burgess immediately radioed a distress call, which was picked up by the Coast Guard. However, high winds at the Otis Air Force Base Coast Guard facility on Cape Cod delayed launch of helicopter 1438 until shortly after noon. Meanwhile, high seas drove back two of the Coast Guard's forty-four-footers after attempting a rescue, injuring a crewman. Rescue would have to come from the cutters *Cape George* and *Cape Cross*, which arrived on scene in time to see "a huge wave lift the bow of the *Poling* over the submerged part of the stern and deposit it on the other side."

Fearing the bow would capsize at any moment, Captain Burgess ordered Selleck to abandon ship and radioed the Coast Guard of his intentions. The *Cape George* picked up Burgess on the first pass, but crewman Selleck was forced to float on his back to keep from drowning and spent nearly fifteen minutes in the icy sea before the *Cape George* could maneuver close enough to rescue him. The rescue came just in time, as life expectancy in thirty-degree water is about twenty minutes. The remaining five members of *Poling*'s crew were stranded on the stern; since the engine room was not taking on water, they did not immediately abandon ship. Angry seas, however, prevented the Coast Guard from shooting a line aboard the half vessel. It was not until the helicopter arrived at 1:30 p.m. that a rescue basket could be lowered to those remaining aboard.

The two-person basket was lowered, and John Gilmete of Jersey City, New Jersey, and ship's cook Joao DaRosa of Providence, Rhode Island, got in. Shortly after leaving the deck, the basket dipped into a cresting wave, at which point DaRosa lost his grip and fell out. "He was with me in the basket," Gilmete said, "But when we came up he just wasn't there." Helicopter pilot Brian Wallace believed DaRosa went into shock after striking the water and drowned. As the stern of the *Poling* drifted closer to the rock-bound coast of Gloucester, seas continued to pound her hull. The three remaining crewmen aboard decided to swim for it and were rescued by the helicopter and waiting cutters; the ship then broke in two. The bow turtled and sank off Eastern Point in 190 feet of water; the stern floated for miles before sinking upright 800 yards off the breakwater in 75 feet of water.

According to the Massachusetts Board of Underwater Archaeological Resources, the *Poling* is an "exempted" shipwreck, which means no permits

Underwater photo of the hatch of the *Chester A. Poling. Courtesy MetroWest Dive Club.*

are needed for exploration or even casual collection of artifacts. The stern is a very popular dive site; usually, there are two mooring buoys maintained by local divers for convenience and safety. According to Keatts, huge waves and surge from the Blizzard of '78 moved the stern into deeper water. Divers will find the *Poling*'s deck at a depth of about seventy-five to one hundred feet in cold water. Divers from the MetroWest Dive Club regularly visit the *Poling* and have an excellent website with underwater photos.

How could an apparently sound, fairly modern vessel, whose crew was knowledgeable of the route and local weather conditions, wreck so dramatically in daylight only thirty-five years ago? For the answer, we will turn to the summary of the Coast Guard Marine Casualty Report published in 1979:

> *During the morning of 10 January 1977, the hull of the coastal tanker CHESTER A. POLING fractured just aft of the pilothouse along the bottom and side shell plating while in the Atlantic Ocean off the coast of Massachusetts. Shortly thereafter, the vessel broke in two and both the bow and stern sections eventually sank. Six of the vessel's seven crew members were rescued by Coast Guard air and sea units while the remaining crewmember was lost at sea…The Commandant has determined that the proximate cause of the casualty was the total structural failure of the hull girder in way of No. 3 cargo tank due to adverse ballast configuration; the combination of ship's speed versus sea conditions encountered; and a reduced sectional modulus of the hull midship structure due to deterioration.*

The report calls for a number of recommendations, including better training of crewmembers in cold water survival and rescue and better equipment such as radios and exposure suits to handle cold water, which was thirty degrees when she sank. The report was critical of the amount and accuracy of the weather forecasts obtained prior to getting underway, including the absence of standard equipment, such as anemometers, barometers and pitch and roll indicators. The report called for better inspections of the ship's structure, including corrosive limits. Finally, the report called for safer operating procedures for ballasting, citing improper sequence as a key contributor to the stress and eventual failure of the hull girder at the number three cargo tank. Importantly, all of these recommendations were reasonable and could have easily been addressed properly prior to getting underway. Why weren't they? Along with weather, ship design and navigation aids, another factor plays a key role with shipwrecks: human error. As we will see with the *Andrea Gail* briefly here and the *Portland* and *Pinthis* in subsequent chapters, the need to get somewhere fast, to stay on schedule, sometimes overrules the caution and prudence that have guided mariners for centuries.

The *Andrea Gail* is the story of a vessel on Grand Banks in pursuit of lucrative swordfish, an underestimated storm and the loss of all onboard. In the fall of 1991, several intense weather patterns combined into what meteorologists described as a "perfect" storm, with winds that reached ninety miles per hour and seas that towered to one hundred feet. The ship was reported overdue; however, bad weather forced the Coast Guard to delay its search briefly. Unfortunately, it would not have made a difference. The six lost crewmen were David Sullivan and Robert Shatford from Gloucester; Billy Tyne, Dale Murphy and Michael Moran from Bradenton Beach, Florida; and Alfred Pierre from New York City. The last recorded words from Captain Billy Tyne were, "She's comin' on, boys, and she's comin' on strong."

The seventy-foot ship was constructed in Panama City, Florida, in 1978 by Eastern Marina Incorporated; its original name was *Miss Penny*. The swordfish long liner and its six-man crew began her final voyage from Gloucester Harbor on September 20, 1991, bound for the Grand Banks off the coast of Newfoundland, Canada. On October 28, as it was halfway home, it ran into hurricane-force winds. A violent nor'easter out of Canada

Andrea Gail in port in Gloucester with the crew's favorite bar, the Crow's Nest, in the background.

merged with the remnants of Hurricane Grace and was squeezed by high pressure from the north back toward the New England coast. The storm was "a deadly combination of three weather fronts comprised of southward-moving arctic energy which collided with a northward-moving tropical storm combined with an offshore Atlantic storm." Bob Case, a meteorologist in the Boston office of the National Weather Service, observed the satellite imagery of three storm systems colliding off New England in late October 1991. Case was shocked when he realized this was a rare and devastating combination of forces. This was truly a once-in-one-hundred-years event, as meteorologists would say, with winds over one hundred miles per hour and waves seventy to one hundred feet high for about seventeen hours.

The *Andrea Gail*, and its sister ship the *Hanna Boden*, were both owned by Robert Brown. In 1991, just days after the ship disappeared, Brown said that the *Andrea Gail* began heading back to Gloucester while the *Hannah Boden* stayed on the fishing grounds. Around nighttime on October 28, the *Andrea Gail* was reported fighting thirty-foot seas and fifty-to eighty-knot winds formed by the nor'easter. At the time, the ship was around 180 miles off of Sable Island. The report came from the New Bedford fishing vessel *Mary T.*, which notified the Canadian Coast Guard in Halifax that it had been in radio contact with the *Andrea Gail*. Near the end of the search for the *Andrea Gail*, there were five airplanes from the United States and Canadian Coast Guards. All together, they searched about 20,000 miles over six days.

Sebastian Junger, author of the 1997 book based on the *Andrea Gail* called *The Perfect Storm*, witnessed the storm's immense power as it hit Gloucester's coast, heaving boulders into shore-side homes and washing out streets and piers. When he learned the storm was one of the worst on record in the region, he spent the next two years gathering information and researching its effects on vessels such as *Andrea Gail*. He interviewed families of the deceased as well as crews from boats that made it through the perfect storm. He examined the layout of the ship, the way the men spent their time in Gloucester, their homeport, and the pressure they were under to capture swordfish. In 2000, a disaster film based on the book was released.

There has been some controversy over how accurate the movie is because no one really knows what happened when the *Andrea Gail* sank. The producers of the movie relied on the knowledge and experience of people such as Richard Haworth, who was captain of the *Andrea Gail* from 1978 until 1986, and Linda Greenlaw, one of the only female swordfish captains on the east coast and survivor of the 1991 storm. She complained about how the movie depicted Billy Tyne and his crew making a conscious decision to go into a storm they knew was dangerous, just to continue swordfishing. Greenlaw stated, "That is not what happened; the *Andrea Gail* was three days into their steam home when the storm hit, and whatever happened to the *Andrea Gail* happened very quickly." Haworth said, "The *Andrea Gail* was always a wet vessel; she took a lot of water on deck. Once fully loaded with fuel, water and fish, she was very low to the water."

Other theories still float around Gloucester. Jack Flaherty, a sixty-four-year-old man with over forty years experience at sea, has one. He used to work on a ship like the *Andrea Gail* that was made from the same builder. His theory is that the *Andrea Gail* may have been low on fuel or had its fuel "muddied" in the rough waters. According to Flaherty, violent movement of the boat can slosh up fuel, bringing up residue, rust or algae; also air could get trapped in the fuel, leading to a stalled engine or engine failure. During the storm, the severe movements of the ship could have also destructed the engine's performance and proficiency.

The tragedy of the *Andrea Gail* fishing vessel made a significant impact on the entire Gloucester community, as well as the families of the victims still in need of closure. In his book, Junger wrote, "If the men on the *Andrea Gail* had simply died, and their bodies were lying in state somewhere, their loved ones could make their goodbyes and get on with their lives; but they didn't die, they disappeared off the face of the earth…" On occasion, Roberta Tyne Smith runs into other family members of the crew at a well-known bar called the Crow's Nest. She remembers clearly how she got the news two decades ago, saying, "I was in the middle of getting ready to go trick-or-treating with my three sons, but life changed dramatically from that day forward." Roberta was most regretful when she knew that Billy would never be able to see his children grow up, because he loved spending every moment with them. Smith recalled how Billy loved to dress up as Santa for Christmas to make a special appearance for his children, nephews and friends' children. She said, "He was so passionate about playing Santa, he bought a suit from Brown's Department Store in Gloucester; that was Billy, always having fun."

The storm left destruction all across New England, New York and New Jersey. Gloucester was severely damaged by the storm, not only in the personal loss but also in property damages. Information from the National Climatic Data Center shows that Massachusetts got the worst of the storm, with an estimated $100 million in damage. New Jersey was hit the second-hardest with about $75 million in damages. The coastal flooding damaged hundreds of homes and businesses and closed roads and airports. Thousands of people were also left without any electricity.

CHAPTER 4

PORTLAND

STELLWAGEN BANK

42° 25 N
70° 30 W

The *Portland* Gale of 1898 was momentous, not only causing a tremendous loss of life, 192 or so from the sinking of the steamer *Portland* alone, but also devastating the coastline of Mass Bay and littering it with hundreds of vessels, fishing gear, flotsam and jetsam. It was such a strong storm that its surge quickly flooded the North River between Marshfield and Scituate. Searching for a more direct path to the bay as the tide ebbed, the North River broke through between Third and Fourth Cliffs, drastically altering the confluence of the North and South Rivers, Herring Brook and spits and closing off her previous exit to the bay three miles south in Marshfield.

There have been many excellent books and articles written about the *Portland* Gale and ship. We have already mentioned Edward R. Snow's writings on the storm and his quest to find the final resting place of the steamer. In 1995, Dave Ball and Fred Freitas wrote *Warnings Ignored—The Story of the Portland Gale—November 1898*. In 2003, Peter Dow Bachelder and Mason Philip Smith added new information, including confirmation of the wreck location, in their book *Four Short Blasts—The Gale of 1898 and the Loss of the Steamer Portland*. Two excellent articles were written by archaeologists at NOAA detailing the life of the steamer and finding the wreck's location. Deborah Marx wrote "Forbidden to Sail—The Steamship *Portland*, 1890–1898," and Matthew Lawrence wrote "Lost and Found: The Search for the *Portland*" in 2004 for the publication *Sea History*. I mention these publications not only to credit those professionals that have added so much to our understanding of this wreck and storm, but also so you can get a sense of the trauma this event caused. Note in the titles above we have the words "warnings," "forbidden," "loss" and "found." This was no ordinary storm.

Finding the wreck was no easy matter either. The specific location—the so-called numbers—is not widely publicized owing to the risk of unauthorized and dangerous diving by those seeking artifacts. Resting at 460 feet, diving on this wreck presents tremendous technical and physical risks. Divers from the group Boston Deep Wrecks are the only divers known to have visited the wreck. Bob Foster, leader of the group, describes the dives in his own words:

I located the wreck in the summer of 2007 but we were diving the Palmer at the time and at 460 FSW the Portland required some serious thinking. I've always viewed this as one of the crown jewels of New England wrecks, but the depth—twice the Andrea Doria—will always make it accessible to only a few. But on August 13, 2008 weather and preparation all came together and a team of 5 divers became the first to visit this historic wreck. Slav Mlch, Dave Faye, Don Morse, Paul Blanchette and myself—supported by Marcie Bilinski and Ricky Simon—dropped down a weighted line we dragged near the wreck and landed between the twin boiler intake stacks and the walking beam. My first view of the wreck was the stacks on my left, and then the walking beam which rises approximately 20 feet above the deck.

Visibility was approximately thirty feet with no ambient light. A large dragger net covers the port paddle wheel and extends partway over the deck and about ten feet above. I was reminded of the depth when one of the UK lights I was using with my video housing imploded at about four hundred feet. The five-hundred-feet rating is obviously a bit generous! There was a significant current across the wreck that prevented us from making a lot of headway, but artifacts littered the deck around the base of the walking beam. Large pitchers, stacked dishes and small brass-framed glass windows were easily identifiable. While the upper decks are completely gone, likely due to the sinking, the main decking is fairly intact. Dave noticed no markings on the plates we saw, but they were also encrusted a great deal. ROV [remotely operated vehicle] footage from NOAA showed stacks of plates as well, but to me, these seemed thicker, suggesting they were not the fine china. Don reported seeing a very large cod inside a hatchway that he estimated at fifty to sixty pounds.

The wreck of the *Portland* contains many of the factors we have discussed so far. We had a devastating storm, a flat-bottom paddlewheel ship that had no business at sea during this storm and a captain who ignored warnings of this approaching storm to "stay on schedule." Let's start with the characteristics of the steamship *Portland*.

In May 1889, the Portland Steam Packet Company contracted with the New England Shipbuilding Company of Bath, Maine, to construct for $240,000 a new 2,284-gross-tonnage vessel for its line between Boston and Portland. Travel by sea at that time was popular, faster and more reliable than travel by land. She was 291 feet in length, 42 feet at the beam and drew an amazingly low 15 feet. The ship had two massive 35-foot paddle wheels and two steam boilers, giving it a top speed of fifteen knots. At a time when many coastal passenger ships were steel-hulled and propeller-driven, the *Portland* was built out of wood with paddlewheels. Why? This new steamer was not built for speed and seaworthiness but to accommodate a great number of passengers in comfort at a reasonable cost. A wooden paddlewheel ship was less expensive to build than a steel-hulled propeller steamship. Sacrificing seaworthiness for comfort and cargo is not unusual. The seven-master *T.W. Lawson*, for example, eliminated steam propulsion for more cargo space, operating on sail power alone. She wrecked in 1907.

In the summer of 1890, the *Portland* arrived at Boston's India Wharf to begin an eight-year run as a reliable mode of transportation between Boston and Portland for businessmen and a popular starting point for vacationers heading to Maine's many resorts. Passengers were promised "the best care

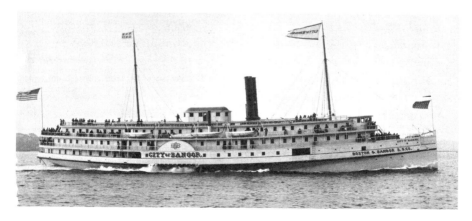

Paddlewheel steamer *City of Bangor* underway, August 1906. Similar in design to the *Portland*, she traveled between Boston Harbor and Rockland, Maine.

Painting of steamer *Portland*, circa 1898.

for the best fare." The berths were white pine with cherry caps. There was a carved and painted globe with the seal of the city of Portland decorating the paddle boxes. The ship was always freshly painted, with polished brass, and full of cheerful passengers. On the morning of November 26, 1898, the *Portland* was moored to its berth at India Wharf while the storm that would change the face of Mass Bay, destroy over 170 vessels and kill over four hundred people was developing.

Weather forecasting at the end of the nineteenth century was not as sophisticated as it is today. From the invention of the barometer, mariners had a good understanding of how changing pressure led to various weather patterns. In fact, log entries of barometric pressure by lighthouse keepers along the South Shore throughout the twenty-sixth started out quite high and dropped precipitously throughout the day, indicating a storm was approaching. A complete understanding of other aspects of weather such as fronts, higher-level winds and water temperatures would not happen until later in the twentieth century when, with the aid of computers and modeling, the interaction of these forces was studied. We know that in those days, weather reports were disseminated to marine railroad and businessmen via the telegraph. The public relied on newspapers, local knowledge and rumors.

According to Ball and Freitas, on the twenty-fourth of November, a cold front swept north from the Gulf of Mexico and south Atlantic coasts and stalled, triggering a storm off the coast of the United States. As that disturbance was organizing, a storm was plunging from the upper Midwest toward the mid Atlantic. Alarmed that these two lows would merge into a dangerous storm, the U.S. Weather Bureau issued the following advisory for the East Coast at 10:30 a.m. on the twenty-sixth of November: "Storm central near Detroit moving east. East to northeast gales with heavy snow tonight. Wind will shift to the west and northwest with much colder temperatures Sunday. Heavy snow indicated for New York and New England tonight. Notify railroad and transportation interests."

Putting out this alert so early in the morning was an indication that meteorologists were concerned with this storm and for good reason. Onboard the *Portland*, Captain Hollis H. Blanchard was readying the ship for a 7:00 p.m. departure under clear skies.

Throughout the day, as Blanchard prepared the ship, the fears of the forecasters were confirmed. By 3:00 p.m., the two fronts had merged off Norfolk, Virginia, and began to

Hollis H. Blanchard, captain of the *Portland* on her final voyage on November 26, 1898.

trek north to New England. Despite these concerns, the public was generally unaware as the sky had only a few clouds and snowfall was still hours away. Snow began to fall at 7:37 p.m. with growing intensity each hour. Some old-timers likened the fierceness of the storm to the gale of April 1851 that destroyed the original Minot's Light. The storm increased in severity during the night, with average wind velocity of fifty and gusts to seventy-two miles per hour. Coupled to these strong winds and heavy snowfall was a full moon that provided above average high tides peaking at 10:30 a.m. on the twenty-seventh of November. There is a saying mariners keep in mind: "It is always better to be on land wishing you were at sea, than at sea wishing you were on land." To those that heeded the warnings and stayed in the harbor, caution and prudence prevailed. To those like Captain Blanchard and the *Portland* that didn't, a heavy price was paid.

Captain Hollis H. Blanchard lived in Westbrook, Maine, with his wife and three children. He was an experienced mariner, working his whole life

Paddlewheel steamer dockside, similar to *Portland*, as it may have been loading passengers in November 1898.

on the sea. He had worked for the Portland Steamship line for ten years, first as a pilot, then a master. He had a reputation as a reliable mariner, experienced with paddlewheels and respectful of the dynamic weather conditions in Mass Bay. According to Ball and Freitas, Blanchard became well known to the men at the U.S. Weather Bureau in Boston as he often solicited their advice before sailing. We know that Blanchard was aware of the approaching storm not only from his relationship with the Weather Bureau staff but also from a conversation he had in the afternoon with Captain Dennison of the *Portland*'s sister ship, the *Bay State*. Dennison had decided to stay in port. At 5:30 p.m., John Liscomb, general manager of the Portland Steamship Company, telephoned for Blanchard, but he could not be found. He left a message telling Blanchard to hold the *Portland* in port until 9:00 p.m., when they would know more about the conditions, and if the weather was worsening, to cancel the trip. At around 5:00 p.m., Blanchard read a telegraph from a weather reporter in New York stating, "Snowing. Wind North West."

Believing he would have somewhat favorable winds from the northwest and the storm would be diminished by the lee of the land, Blanchard and the *Portland* departed on schedule at 7:00 p.m. At 7:20 p.m., she was seen by the keeper of the Deer Island Light and traded whistles with the *Kennebec*, which was returning to the safety of Boston Harbor. Several other vessels heading back to Boston Harbor reported seeing the *Portland* passing Graves

Light, fully expecting her to turn back. The snow began to intensify at 8:00 p.m., and by 9:00 p.m., she was spotted on schedule off Bass Rocks southwest of Thatcher's Island—not too far from where the *Chester A. Poling* would go down seventy-one years later—by Master William Thomas in a schooner racing back to the safety of Gloucester Harbor. The steamer was sighted at 11:00 p.m. southwest of Thatcher's Island by the schooner *Grayling*. The visibility was so poor that the two vessels nearly collided, with the *Portland* veering at the last minute. The master of the *Grayling* reported the steamer rolling and pitching badly. The last sighting was at 11:45 p.m., fourteen miles southeast of Eastern Point, and far off course, by Captain Edgar Randall who reported seeing a paddle-steamer with a badly damaged superstructure. No one knows how she went down. Was it from engine failure, massive waves or a stress fracture?

The next day, bodies strapped in life belts and debris with the *Portland*'s mark started washing up on the beaches inside the Cape. Approximately 40 of the 192 or so people aboard washed ashore; as there was no manifest left behind, it is unclear the exact number. We do know half of the ship's crew and several passengers were black and hailed from *Portland*, many from the same church. Their deaths devastated the community financially and personally, especially as most families had recently gathered to celebrate Thanksgiving.

Why Captain Blanchard got underway when most stayed is an open question. He was well known as a cautious seafaring man. Perhaps it was this cautious reputation that led to his recklessness that evening. According to one report, Blanchard's superiors felt he was "too cautious in view of the fact that the alternate and competitive route would be by rail." It was possible Blanchard wanted to demonstrate he was bold, especially to his rival Dennison, captain of the sister ship *Bay State*, and "proudly steam into *Portland* harbor Sunday morning and show…that he could take his ship through any storm without fear." A report from a passenger that spoke with Blanchard on the twenty-sixth but changed her mind and did not board the ill-fated vessel said Blanchard was looking forward to spending time with his daughter in Portland and may have been planning a "coming out party" for her on Sunday.

The storm was devastating from New York to Maine. According to Bachelder and Smith, from one end of the Cape to the other, the stories were the same. Nine wharves along Provincetown blew down, as did twenty-one buildings inland. Along the South Shore from Plymouth to Hull, massive storm surge swept over these coastal towns. Of the fourteen cottages lining Plymouth

Beach, only two survived. In Scituate Sand Hills, more than sixty cottages were damaged or destroyed. At Hingham Cove, all the roads close to the steamboat wharf were in two feet of water. A *Boston Globe* reporter trying to describe the damage along Nantasket Beach remarked: "…standing by the Atlantic House and looking up the beach, everything is seen to be destroyed as far as the eye can reach…excepting the Hotel Nantasket. The Rockland Café is gone and… many of the smaller hotels along the beach will be found to be wrecked."

The southern coast of Scituate is marked by four distinct drumlins running from First Cliff on the northern end of the coast down to Fourth Cliff in the southern end. Prior to the *Portland* Gale, the North River flowed south between Fourth Cliff and Marshfield, joining the South River and entering the ocean three miles south. During the storm, a thin strip of beach, which connected Third Cliff to Fourth Cliff, was breached by the river, leaving Fourth Cliff an island. Eventually the old inlet silted in, forcing the South River to flow north between Marshfield and Fourth Cliff, where it now joins the North River to enter the ocean between Third and Fourth Cliffs. Although Fourth Cliff is now connected by land to Marshfield north of Rexhame Beach, there are no roads across the old inlet. As a result, Fourth Cliff and the rest of the Humarock part of Scituate are only accessible via Marshfield. The change to the course of the North River also increased the

Sandy road between Third and Fourth Cliffs prior to November 1898. As the tide ebbed during the *Portland* Gale, the North River broke through between the cliffs and created a new inlet.

salinity of the large marsh area surrounding the current outlet, resulting in the loss of the valuable salt haying business.

North of the city, Revere's shoreline took on what was reported as "a strange, wild and woebegone appearance." At Salem, twenty inches of snow and wind caused large trees to come crashing down, severing power and phone lines. Around Gloucester, the mighty gusts collapsed the new brick and iron Gloucester Street Railway storage house, demolishing seventeen new and four older streetcars. The *Boston Globe* evening edition November twenty-eighth headline read: "Globe Extra! 170 vessels. Graves in the Vasty Deep for Scores of Seamen All Along the New England Coast, and the Fear is That the List Will be Monumental—Lives Lost in This Harbor Are Many—Trying to Save Craft in Jeopardy."

Whenever there are storms, there will be brave people trying to save those in peril, and the *Portland* Gale proved no different. Before we get to the specific acts of bravery that terrible weekend, let's take a look at how this lifesaving force started. Near the turn of the eighteenth century, it had become obvious that a dedicated group of lifesavers had to be established, prompted most likely by a series of fatal wrecks on the East Coast. Several wealthy concerned citizens organized the Humane Society of the Commonwealth of Massachusetts in 1785 to meet this need. In 1792, six huts of refuge were built, and in 1807, the society constructed the first station fitted with a lifeboat on the coast of Cohasset. By 1845, there were eighteen stations located at critical points along the most desolate and dangerous sections of Mass Bay. They were manned by volunteers and equipped with boats and line-throwing guns such as was used to rescue the crew of the *Etrusco* a century later. The Humane Society was precursor to the U.S. Lifesaving Service, which eventually became the U.S. Coast Guard in 1915.

The volunteer that most exemplifies the lifesaving service was Joshua James. Born in 1826 in Hull, he was called a "great caretaker" by his siblings and was reared by his sister Catherine after their mother and baby sister drowned in the sinking of the *Hepzibah* on April 3, 1837. Returning from Boston through Hull's Gut, the sloop was engulfed by a sudden squall and thrown on her beam-ends. She filled with water and sank before Mrs. James and her baby daughter trapped below in a cabin could be rescued. This event had an important influence in shaping Joshua's career as a lifesaver. "Ever after that," said his sister, "he seemed to be scanning the sea in quest of imperiled lives." A natural seaman, Joshua started going to sea early in life with his father and brothers. On one occasion, while he was sailing a yacht in dense fog, all bearings apparently lost, someone asked him where they were.

"We are just off Long Island head," he replied. "How can you tell that?" he was asked. "I can hear the land talk," he replied.

Joshua's lifesaving career began in 1842 when he joined the Massachusetts Humane Society in the rescue of the *Harding's Ledge*. He went on to become famous as the commander of civilian lifesaving crews in the nineteenth century and was involved in so many rescues over the years that a special silver medal was struck for him by the Humane Society in 1886, for brave and faithful service for more than forty years. The report said,

> *During this time, he assisted in saving over 100 lives. During* The *Portland* Gale, *he assisted in the rescue of two survivors from two vessels dashed upon Toddy Rocks; rescued 7 men via breeches buoy from a 3-masted schooner; opened the station to a family whose home was threatened by the storm; assisted in the rescue of 5 men from a beached barge; assisted in the rescue of three men from an unnamed schooner; and assisted in the rescue of three men from Black Rock.*

During the height of the *Portland* Gale, men like Joshua James were busy all over the bay from North Scituate to Fourth Cliff, from Point Allerton to Brant Rock and Gurnet Stations, from Cape Ann to Race Point. Although not successful, the rescue efforts of the pilot boat *Columbia* give a glimpse into these heroics. In 1898, there were eight pilot boats that searched the waters off Boston for incoming vessels requiring a pilot to navigate them past the harbor's many hazards. One of these vessels, the *Columbia*, eighty-five feet long and eighty-nine tons, was a particularly pleasing boat with a clipper-type stern. Manned by a crew of five, with four pilots ready to board incoming ships, she was also considered a "lucky" vessel and had the number two stitched to her sail. The *Columbia* had gone on station outside Boston Harbor a few days before the gale hit. Being far offshore, she may not have been fully aware of the approaching disaster but certainly knew by Saturday evening that the weather was turning ugly. According to Ball and Freitas, hour by hour the *Columbia* was driven closer to the Scituate shore, eventually dropping two anchors. Brought ashore no doubt by Sunday's morning's high tide, the *Columbia* wrecked on Cedar Point with the loss of all crewmembers.

Testimony by lifesaving serviceman Richard Tobin who passed by the spot where the *Columbia* crashed ashore stated:

> *I went down to the beach to the key post three miles from the station. When I started there was much wreckage on the beach, and the seas were coming*

over with such force that I was washed into Mesquashcut Pond. It was blowing so hard that I was obliged to kneel down at times to get my breath. It was a hurricane from the northeast, and snowing so that I could not see any distance offshore. I kept on, and I had to take the fields back to the beach. Then I was able to make better progress, and at last reached the post and then started to return. I warned a number of people in houses nearby that they had better seek safety elsewhere—to a safe place in another house, and also assisted a fisherman to haul his boats away from the danger. When I was through with these things I started for the station and had to travel along the fields, it being impossible to keep on the beach. I got back to the station a little after half passed three in the afternoon.

The Saturday midnight patrols did not begin until 1:00 a.m. due to high surf. Surfman John Curran on the 4:00 a.m. sunrise patrol came upon the *Columbia* at the neck of Cedar Point. She was driven high on the beach, her foremast gone, the starboard side badly damaged, the anchor chains extended and anchors missing. The body of one crewman lay in the hold. The surfman hurried back to the station and alerted George Brown, keeper, who immediately dispatched three more surfmen to the scene, where four more bodies were found. The entire crew of the *Columbia* was lost, most likely drowning before she reached the beach. Interestingly, Otis Barker purchased

Helm of the *Portland* recovered on the beach at Race Point, Provincetown, in November 1898.

the *Columbia* hulk shortly after the storm and turned it in to a cottage. It remained on the beach as a tourist attraction until the early 1930s, when the rotted structure was removed.

Some consequences of the 1898 storm were immediate and some carried on for several years, including the location of the *Portland* wreck, which was not confirmed until 2002. Over 170 vessels and four hundred lives were lost in less than twenty-four hours. A week following the storm, Fran Wellock, a veteran pilot captain, gave his thoughts to a reporter as to how the *Portland* Gale compared to other storms, particularly the Minot's Light Gale of 1851:

> *I never want to have to go through another such experience as [I] had to endure on the pilot boat Minerva from 3 to 5 am Sunday morning, when the gale was at its height. We were anchored in President's Roads in outer Boston Harbor, and the strength of our chains and anchors was our salvation. I have been out in gales before of course, but none of them are worth speaking of in comparison to this one.*

The search for the *Portland* wreck began once the seas calmed with a report from the ship Bay State that no trace of the steamer was seen. Two weeks after its sinking, the *Boston Globe* sponsored an expedition to determine if the steamer's remains rested on a sandbar running just offshore the northernmost end of Cape Cod. Using chains to drag the area, a U.S. naval officer proved it was not the remains of the *Portland*. Edward Rowe Snow believed the *Portland* survived the storm for twenty-four hours, not sinking until Sunday night, the twenty-seventh, though it is doubtful she had enough fuel to last that long. Most captains and pilots at the time believed Blanchard made a run for deeper water, as you'll remember the *Etrusco* attempted to do in 1956. For nearly eighty years, rumors of its whereabouts have persisted, mostly egged on by a fishing vessel or two snagging its nets on something deep below or pulling up some artifact apparently from the *Portland*. After hearing of a fishing boat pulling up pottery from the *Portland* in 1924, Edward Rowe Snow surmised the *Portland* sank several miles north of Race Point, organized a diving expedition and dedicated a monument in 1945 to the nearly two hundred crewmembers and passengers that perished. In 1978, divers from the Historical Maritime Group of New England (HMGNE) located the wreck Snow thought was the *Portland* and proved that it was not.

Determined to find the *Portland*'s final resting place, John Fish of the HMGNE decided to look in a new direction by plotting where *Portland*'s debris had washed up on Cape Cod. Consulting with Richard Limeburner

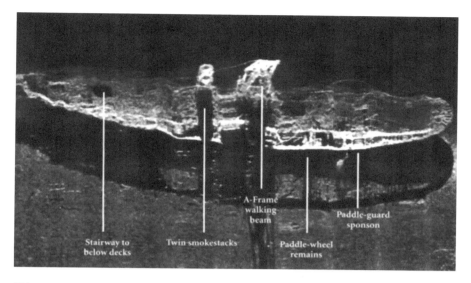

Sidescan sonar of the Portland wreck, 460 feet below the surface between Cape Ann and Race Point in the Stellwagen Bank. *Courtesy NOAA.*

of the Woods Hole Oceanographic Institution, Fish moved the search area farther north, closer to where the *Portland* was last sighted and closer to where fishermen first reported getting their nets snagged. After three more years of searching, HMGNE's side-scan sonar finally returned the first acoustic images of *Portland* in the fall of 1988 and the following summer. Subsequent photos of the engine walking beam and outer hull further confirmed the location of the wreck. Fish and his associates chose not to publicly disclose the vessel's position for fear that others might attempt to gain salvage rights.

It was not until four years later with the establishment in 1992 of the Stellwagen Bank National Marine Sanctuary—which covered and protected the area where the *Portland* went down—that the owners of the *Portland's* "numbers" started to feel comfortable divulging its location. In the spring of 2002, the location of the wreck was provided to the sanctuary. In the summer, the sanctuary team recorded side-scan sonar images and underwater video of the wreck that confirmed its identity, sitting upright on the ocean floor off Cape Ann. According to Lawrence, the circumstances that caused the *Portland* to sink after battling the wind and waves for over twelve hours have not been conclusively determined; however, the underwater images of the *Portland's* hull reveal it to be largely intact. Most telling, nearly all the vessel's superstructure is missing, hinting at the tremendous forces exerted on the vessel during its final moments.

CHAPTER 5

SHANNON-CHESAPEAKE
SIX LEAGUES OFF BOSTON LIGHT

42° 20 N
70° 33 W

Eleven miles off the coast of Scituate and around twenty-one miles—six leagues—from Boston Light, not too far from where the *Portland* sank in 1898, the British warship *Shannon* and the American warship *Chesapeake* fought in the summer of 1813. While the battle ended with neither of the combatants sinking to the ocean floor, there is no doubt the USS *Chesapeake* was a bloody wreck.

Earlier in the day on June 1, 1813, Captain James Lawrence of the USS *Chesapeake*, a thirty-eight-gun frigate, had seemingly answered the challenge of his rival, Captain P.B.V. Broke of the British frigate *Shannon*, and departed Boston Harbor for battle. Lawrence, who had successfully captained the sloop *Hornet* in 1812, had recently taken charge of the *Chesapeake*. Both of these naval warriors were respected in the United States, Great Britain and Canada. Meeting off Scituate with a green crew, Lawrence was unable to match the superior gunnery of the *Shannon* and the ships were lashed together. Captain Broke and fifty of his men rushed onboard and started fierce hand-to-hand combat for possession of the gangway. Many of the *Chesapeake*'s crewmembers were driven into the hold.

Captain Lawrence was mortally wounded, and his ship was captured and towed to Halifax, Nova Scotia. His final words live on: "The colors shall wave while I live; tell the men to fire faster and don't give up the ship!" Broke also was wounded in the head and, prior to passing out, inquired about Lawrence. Hearing he was mortally wounded, Broke sent his own

USS *Chesapeake* as she may have looked pierside at the Boston Navy Yard in the days prior to the battle. *Michelle Garcia, illustrator.*

surgeon to take care of him, but Lawrence died on the way to port. Broke's second in command, Lieutenant Wallis, returned both ships to British naval headquarters. The people of Halifax gathered at the piers as both ships came into the harbor but, out of respect for the *Chesapeake* and her now deceased captain, remained silent. Interestingly, a year later the HMS *Bulwark* attempted to raze the town of Scituate but was scared away by Abigail and Rebecca Bates, who hid behind a sand dune near the lighthouse and played the fife and drum, as any regiment would. Broke recovered, returned to England and was knighted.

Thousands on the South Shore and some up north in Nahant and Marblehead saw the quick fifteen-minute battle in the distance and smelled the smoke from the cannons; people from the town of Canton watched from the top of the Blue Hills. Three frightened boys from the North River in Scituate, Perez Hatch, Thomas Mitchell and Thomas Stetson, had an even better view. Captured and released by the *Shannon* after their fishing boat had been inspected, they watched the battle from their small boat. To the thousands of spectators watching, the battle was devastating to them and their young county. To keep this battle in the proper perspective, we need to understand the events leading up to the War of 1812, including the wreck of Oliver Hazard Perry's ship *Revenge* and his subsequent victory as the "Hero of Lake Erie."

When the British lost the Revolutionary War, they also lost access to the large American naval labor force. The Royal Navy sailed worldwide, and

Painting of the *Shannon-Chesapeake* battle on June 1, 1813. *Courtesy National Archives.*

its labor needs were intense, which they solved by going into the streets, saloons and homes of port cities and capturing potential sailors. It often categorized impressed sailors as British subjects, no matter their origins. Even with impressments, general relations between the United States and Great Britain were civil, though strained. British ships regularly called at American ports for repair and supplies, and Americans were still in touch with their British origins.

A solution to the problem lay in the determination by President George Washington and the Congress in 1794 to build six frigates that would defend American interests at sea and ultimately form the foundation of the United States Navy. The *Chesapeake* was one of those six—along with *Constellation, Constitution, Congress, President* and *United States*—*and considered* unlucky since her name was the only one of the six not associated with a symbol of the new American democracy. The two shipbuilders most responsible for her design and construction—Joshua Humphreys and Josiah Fox—apparently despised each other. Shipbuilders often found that materials meant for her construction were given instead to other frigates. This lack of respect for the *Chesapeake* seemed to come to a head in 1807 when she was attacked without provocation by the British, who refused to take her as a prize of battle.

In 1807, the *Chesapeake* set out from Hampton Roads to the Mediterranean with her officers and crew, a family and their servants, an Italian Marine band and their instruments and a horse. Commodore James Barron had no reason to expect, and the ship was not yet prepared for, what happened next. Officers of the HMS *Leopard* made a friendly approach to the *Chesapeake* and, once aboard, demanded that Barron give up four of his sailors believed to be British subjects. Barron refused, and when the British officers returned to their ship, the *Chesapeake* was immediately shot across the bow, followed by four crushing broadsides. With no means to fight back, Barron raised a flag of surrender and, following the code of battle, offered the *Chesapeake* as a prize. The offer was spurned by the *Leopard*, but the four sailors were taken prisoner. The unprovoked attack on the *Chesapeake* awakened an anti-British rage among Americans and was a catalyst for a new determination that the United States was a sovereign nation that needed to defend itself with a strong navy.

By 1811, the British had conceded that the 1807 attack on the *Chesapeake* had been a mistake and made reparations. But Great Britain was still interfering with American commerce on the seas, and impressments or "the press" was still the practice. War with Great Britain was also seen by some, controversially, as an opportunity for the United States to expand into British-controlled Canada. On June 1, President Madison sent a war message to Congress, which passed after debate, and declared war on the eighteenth. The next day, the British revoked the Orders of Council, which was the key reason for the United States declaring war. However, communication of this did not reach the United States quickly, and fighting began. In the first year of the war, U.S. frigates scored victories over the Royal Navy that were surprising, even to the Americans, and dispiriting for the British, who sorely needed a victory at sea. By May 1813, the British were desperate to revenge the defeats of the *Macedonian*, *Guerrière*, *Peacock* and *Java*.

On the morning of June 1, Captain Broke sent a challenge to Captain James Lawrence, who had been recently transferred to the *Chesapeake*, in which he said:

> *I request that you will do me the favor to meet the Shannon ship to ship, to try the fortune of our respective flags...I will send all other ships beyond the power of interfering with us, and meet you whenever it is most agreeable to you...I will warn you should any of my friends be too nigh...or I would sail with you, under a flag of truce, to any place you think safest from our cruisers, hauling it down when fair to begin hostilities...You will feel it as a compliment if I say that the result of our meeting may be the most*

HMS *Leopard* visiting the USS *Chesapeake* in 1807. *Courtesy National Archives.*

grateful service I can render to my country; and I doubt not that you, equally confident of success, will feel convinced that it is only by repeated triumphs, in even combats, that your little navy can now hope to console your country for the loss of that trade it can no longer protect.

This was certainly a coldblooded challenge but one that was never received, as the *Chesapeake* sailed that morning, the same day letter was sent.

Prior to becoming president, Theodore Roosevelt wrote an excellent account of the battle in his book Naval *War of 1812*. As you will note, the *Chesapeake* gave away a clear advantage when she failed to make use of her position astern of the *Shannon*:

At midday of June 1, 1813, the Chesapeake weighed anchor, stood out of Boston Harbor, and at 1 P.M. rounded the Lighthouse. The Shannon stood off under easy sail, and at 3:40 hauled up and reefed topsails. At 4 p.m., she again bore away with her foresail brailed up, and her maintopsail braced flat and shivering, that the Chesapeake might overtake her. An hour later, Boston Lighthouse bearing west distant about six leagues, she again hauled up, with her head to the southeast, and lay to under topsails, topgallantsails, jib, and spanker...

At 5:25 the Chesapeake hauled up her foresail, and, with three ensigns flying, steered straight for the Shannon's starboard quarter. Broke was afraid that Lawrence would pass under the Shannon's stern, rake her, and engage her on the quarter; but either overlooking or waiving this advantage, the American captain luffed up within fifty yard, upon the Shannon's starboard quarter, and squared his mainyard.

On board the Shannon the captain of the 14th gun, William Mindham, had been ordered not to fire till it bore into the second main-deck port forward; at 5:50 it was fired, and then the other guns in quick succession from aft forward, the Chesapeake replying with her whole broadside. At 5:53 Lawrence, finding he was forging ahead, hauled up a little. The Chesapeake's broadsides were doing great damage, but she herself was suffering even more than her foe; the men in the Shannon's tops could hardly see the deck of the American frigate through the cloud of splinters, hammocks, and other wreck that was flying across it.

Man after man was killed at the wheel; the fourth lieutenant, the master, and the boatswain were slain; and at 5:56, having had her jib sheet and foretop-sail tie shot away, and her spanker brails loosened so that the sail blew out, the Chesapeake came up into the wind somewhat, so as to expose her quarter to her antagonist's broadside, which beat in her stem-ports and swept the men from the after guns. One of the arm-chests on the quarter-deck was blown up by a hand-grenade thrown from the Shannon.

The Shannon's crew had suffered severely, but not the least panic or disorder existed among them. Broke ran forward, and seeing his foes flinching from the quarter-deck guns, he ordered the ships to be lashed together, the great guns to cease firing, and the boarders to be called. The boatswain, who had fought in Rodney's action, set about fastening the vessels together, which the grim veteran succeeded in doing, though his right arm was literally hacked off by a blow from a cutlass. All was confusion and dismay on board the Chesapeake. Lieutenant Ludlow had been mortally wounded and carried below; Lawrence himself,

Coming out of Boston Harbor on the morning of June 1, 1813, the *Chesapeake* soon spotted the *Shannon* north near Nahant. She then sailed to a point east of Boston Light and commenced fighting at 5:50 p.m. Within fifteen minutes, it was over, with *Shannon* victorious and crowds from Scituate to Marblehead shocked.

> *while standing on the quarter-deck, fatally conspicuous by his full-dress uniform, and commanding stature, was shot down, as the vessels closed, by Lieutenant Law of the British marines. He fell dying, and was carried below, exclaiming: "Don't give up the ship"—a phrase that has since become proverbial among his countrymen.*

Depiction of hand-to-hand combat on the USS *Constitution*, which is similar to how her sister ship the *Chesapeake* would have looked during her fight with the *Shannon*. *Courtesy the Marine Art of J. Clary, www.jclary.com.*

In the short span of fifteen minutes, the *Chesapeake* had been hit 362 times, sixty-one of her crew had been killed and eighty-five wounded, while the *Shannon* had been struck 158 times and eighty-three of her seamen were dead or disabled. To the dismay and surprise of the people on the shore of Mass Bay, the English flag was soon seen at the masthead of the *Chesapeake*. According to news reports, Bostonians were so sure of a victory that they had prepared a banquet, and Broke and his officers were to have been invited. Instead they had to watch their ship being carried away within sight of Boston Light, and those who came out in their vessels had to steer their way sadly back to Boston. The two ships then started for Halifax, their decks strewn with the dead and dying, the commander of one unconscious and the other dying. Lawrence died on the fifth of June and was buried in Halifax with full honors.

Roosevelt claimed the *Chesapeake* loss was due to poor training:

> *Neither ship had lost a spar, but all the lower masts, especially the two mizzenmasts, were badly wounded. American ships like the Chesapeake were fond of using bar shot, which were of very questionable benefit, being useless against a ship's hull. It is thus seen that the Shannon received from shot alone*

Depiction of the *Shannon-Chesapeake* battle. *Michelle Garcia, illustrator.*

*only about half the damage the Chesapeake did; the latter was thoroughly
beaten at the guns, in spite of what some American authors say to the contrary.
And her victory was not in the slightest degree to be attributed to, though it may
have been slightly hastened by accident. Training and discipline won the victory,
as often before; only in this instance the training and discipline were against us.*

An investigation revealed five traitors among the crew of the *Chesapeake*
that allowed naval signals to fall into the hands of the enemy; a special
committee was formed to select a new code.

As she was taken to England, she ceased to be the USS *Chesapeake* and
became the HMS *Chesapeake*. She was studied by her captors and sailed under
the British flag. The HMS *Chesapeake* was spotted back in her namesake bay
on April 13, 1814, as part of a British flotilla. In subsequent years, she was
probably a stores ship at Portsmouth, England. The War of 1812 ended with
the Treaty of Ghent in 1814, and the Napoleonic Wars between Britain and
France ended in 1815. England, an island nation, had always recycled its
basic materials. Its fleets of wooden sailing ships were of better use broken
up into timbers and boards for the building of houses, barns, churches and
furniture. The USS/HMS *Chesapeake*, built in Portsmouth, Virginia, was

SUPERIOR SHIP TIMBER.

*To Gentlemen, Farmers, Ship and House Buil-
ders, Smiths, and Others:*

THE HULLS of his Majesty's late Ships, CHESAPEAKE and CHERUB, are now breaking up at Pesthouse, near Portsea, where there is for Sale, a very large quantity of OAK and FIR TIMBER, of most excellent quality, and well worth the attention of any person; consisting of 150 Oak and Fir Beams, of the following sizes—5 by 7, 7 by 9, 8 by 10, 12 by 15, from 20 to 40 feet long; Oak and Fir Plank 2½, 3, 4, 5, 6, and 7 inches of long lengths, from 40 to 70 feet, Floors, Futticks, Top Timbers, Knees, Carlins, Ledges, Cabin Fittings, and a larger and more supe-rior assortment of Ship Timber, than was ever before offered to the Public.

Also, an excellent double Capstan, about 30 Tons of Swedish Iron, Spikes, Bolts, and about 30 Iron Knees.

The above may be Shipped free of expence, being close to the water.—For particulars, enquire of Jo-seph Pushman and Co. on the Premises.

Newspaper article in 1819 offering timber from the derelict HMS *Chesapeake*.

broken up in Portsmouth, England, in 1819. Her timbers, cut from the forests of coastal North America, were advertised for sale in a British newspaper.

A friend of Lawrence's, Captain George Crowninshield fitted out the ship *Henry* at his own expense to recover Lawrence's remains and succeeded in bringing them back to Salem, where the funeral was held. Crowninshield hailed from the famous Marblehead family of naval architects; his grandson B.B. Crowninshield would go on to design the world's only seven-masted schooner, the *T.W. Lawson*, in 1901. Congress eventually voted a pension to Lawrence's wife. But the story does not end here. The death of Captain Lawrence greatly affected another friend, Oliver Hazard Perry, and his devotion to Lawrence changed the course of the War of 1812.

Oliver Hazard Perry was born in 1785 in South Kingstown, Rhode Island, the son of U.S. Navy captain Christopher Raymond Perry and Sarah Wallace Alexander, a direct descendant of William Wallace, a Scottish knight and hero of the War for Scottish Independence and older brother to Commodore Matthew Calbraith Perry, who compelled the opening of Japan to the West by threat of force. As a boy, Perry lived in Rhode Island, sailing ships in anticipation of his future career as an officer in the U.S. Navy. He was educated in Newport, Rhode Island, and at the age of thirteen was appointed a midshipman in the U.S. Navy on April 7, 1799. During the quasi-war with France, he was assigned to his father's frigate, the USS *General Greene*.

Beginning in 1806, he commanded the fourteen-gun schooner USS *Revenge* engaging in patrol duties to enforce the Embargo Act, as well as a successful raid to regain a U.S. ship held in Spanish territory in Florida. The *Revenge* sank on the reefs off Watch Hill on January 8, 1811, while surveying southern New England harbors, including New London. The ensuing court-martial exonerated Perry, placing blame instead on the ship's pilot. Following the court-martial, Perry was given a leave of absence from the navy. During that period, he learned of the battle of the *Shannon* and *Chesapeake* in the summer of 1813 and the death of his longtime good friend Captain James Lawrence. Devastated by his friend's death, he vowed to name his next ship after him and fly a battle flag with his famous final words, "Don't give up the ship!"

Perry wasn't retired long and soon was given command of U.S. naval forces on Lake Erie. On September 10, 1813, Perry's command fought a successful fleet action against a task force of the Royal Navy in the Battle of Lake Erie. Master Commandant Perry, his 540 seamen and nine vessels took on the British of Commander Heriot Barclay and his squadron of six ships and 450 men. It was at the outset of this battle that Perry famously said, "If a victory is to be gained, I will gain it." Initially, the exchange of gunfire favored the British. Perry's flagship, the USS *Lawrence*, was so severely disabled in the encounter that Commander Barclay thought Perry would surrender and sent a small boat to request the American vessel pull down its flag. Faithful to the words of his battle flag, "Don't give up the ship," Perry ordered the crippled *Lawrence* to fire a final salvo and then had his men row him a half mile through heavy gunfire to transfer his command to the USS *Niagara*.

Once aboard, Perry dispatched the *Niagara*'s commander, Captain Jesse Elliot, to bring the other schooners into closer action while he steered the *Niagara* toward the damaged British ships. Breaking through the British line, the American force pounded Barclay's ships until they could offer no effective resistance and surrendered. Although he had won the battle aboard the *Niagara*, he received the British surrender on the deck of the recaptured *Lawrence* to allow the British to see the terrible price his men had paid. Perry's battle report to General William Henry Harrison was famously brief: "We have met the enemy and they are ours; two ships, two brigs, one schooner and one sloop." This was the first time in history that an entire British naval squadron had surrendered, and every captured ship was successfully returned to Presque Isle. The saying "Don't give up the ship" is now the battle cry of the U.S. Navy.

In August 2005, Charles Buffum and Craig Harger discovered the wreck of Perry's ship *Revenge* but kept it secret until 2011—two centuries after it sank— as they continued to explore the area and make additional finds. Since then, they have found four more forty-two-inch-long cannons, an anchor, canister shot and other metal objects they believe are from the *Revenge*. Perry faced a court-martial over the wreck but was eventually exonerated as blame fell on the ship's pilot. Because of the incident, however, the formerly fast-rising captain could not get command of a ship battling the British along the eastern seaboard. He had to settle for the less glamorous position of commanding a fleet of warships in the Great Lakes. His luck changed in 1813, however, as the fleet under his command defeated the British in the Battle of Lake Erie

The divers say the wreck changed the course of history because Perry likely would not have been sent to Lake Erie otherwise. Buffum said he had been interested in finding the remains of the *Revenge* ever since his mother several years ago gave him the book *Shipwrecks on the Shores of Westerly*. The book includes Perry's account of the wreck, which happened when it hit a reef in a storm in heavy fog off Watch Hill in Westerly, Rhode Island, as Perry was bringing the ship from Newport to New London, Connecticut. "I always thought to myself we ought to go out and have a look and just see if there's anything left," Buffum said. The two, along with a third man, Mike Fournier, set out to find it with the aid of a metal detector. After several dives, they came across a cannon, then another. The navy has a right to salvage its shipwrecks; the divers have contacted the Naval History and Heritage Command, which oversees such operations, in hopes the navy will salvage the remains. If the navy does not, they said they hope to raise the money for a salvage operation so the artifacts can be displayed at a historical society.

Two towns claim a special right to the saying "Don't give up the ship": Scituate, Massachusetts, where most people viewed the *Shannon-Chesapeake* battle when the famous words were first spoken, and Sandusky, Ohio, closest to where Oliver Hazard Perry fought the Battle of Lake Erie. Sandusky will celebrate on September 7, 2013, the exact week of the bicentennial of the battle. Scituate will also be celebrating as part of the 375th anniversary of the town founding. Scituate historian Mat Brown said, "We did some research and sure enough, it was eleven miles off the coast so people would have seen it. We thought people ought to know this about Scituate—which it's very close to this battle site from a very bloody war. 'Don't give up the ship' is very much a part of the U.S. Navy and very much a part of Scituate."

CHAPTER 6

SUBMARINE *S-4*

PROVINCETOWN

42° 02.12N
70° 19.35W

As we have discussed, ships wreck for many reasons, such as bad weather, poor navigation aids, equipment and skills, poor ship design and structural deficiencies, bad judgment and war. Sometimes, though, wrecks happen because of bad luck, or what is sometimes referred to as an act of God. I remember leaving the Philippines in 1984 aboard the USS *Kirk*, a Knox-class frigate. Without warning, in calm seas, we were knocked over by a single thirty-foot rogue wave. Prior to that, I would not have believed these odd black swan events could happen; I believe it now.

Given the long hours over the horizon away from land, away from family, at the mercy of storms and doldrums, alongside dangerous reefs, shoals and sea animals, it is no wonder many mariners are superstitious. The word "albatross" is sometimes used metaphorically to mean a psychological burden that feels like a curse. It is an allusion to Samuel Taylor Coleridge's poem "The Rime of the Ancient Mariner." In the poem, an albatross starts to follow a ship—being followed by an albatross was generally considered good luck. However, the protagonist mariner shoots the albatross with a crossbow, which is considered bad luck; the ship, indeed, suffers terrible mishaps. To punish him, his shipmates make him wear the dead albatross around his neck until they all die from the curse. Thus the albatross can be both an omen of good or bad luck, as well as a metaphor for a burden to be carried. The symbolism used in the Coleridge poem is its highlight:

Ah! well a-day! what evil looks
Had I from old and young!
Instead of the cross, the Albatross
About my neck was hung.

To avoid mishaps and bring good luck, sailors and fishermen had many idiosyncrasies. For example, a conscientious seafarer would never step on or off a ship by leading with the left foot. Many mariners strive to keep a content and well-fed black cat onboard during their voyages. A pod of dolphins following the wake of a vessel is thought to be a sign of good luck, while malingering schools of sharks can only spell doom. Leaving port on Friday is poor form as Christ was crucified on Good Friday. Legend has it the British Navy fought this superstition to the point that they laid the keel of a warship on a Friday, launched the vessel on another Friday, named the craft HMS *Friday* and sailed it out of port for the first time on Friday. As you could guess, it never made it back to the harbor again. Another widespread superstition forbids whistling in the wheelhouse or anywhere onboard for that matter. Whistling onboard will raise a gale, hence the phrase "whistling up a storm."

Several shipwrecks near Provincetown are good examples of bad luck ships or, in one case, a bad luck submarine. Located at the tip of Cape Cod, Provincetown, sometimes called P-Town, is known for its beaches, harbor, fishing, artists and tourist industry. It is also known for its strong winds, riptides and shoals that have captured thousands of ships. Provincetown was originally settled by the Nauset tribe; in 1620, the Pilgrims signed the Mayflower Compact when they arrived at the harbor. They agreed to build a self-governing community and then came ashore at the west end. Though the Pilgrims soon left P-Town and settled across the bay in Plymouth, others came and settled the area, though the population remained small through most of the eighteenth century. Following the American Revolution, however, it grew rapidly as a fishing and whaling center with an excellent harbor. It was also an excellent location for running rum.

In 1920, the Liquor Prohibition Amendment, which prohibited the manufacture, sale, transportation, importation or exportation of intoxicating liquors, came into effect. Prohibition gave rise to the smuggling of illicit liquor into the United States. Rumrunning started when ships from the western Bahamas transported cheap Caribbean rum to Florida smugglers. If vessels stayed in international waters, beyond the rum line, set at three miles off the coast (later increased to twelve miles in 1924), authorities such as the Coast Guard could not apprehend the smugglers. Searching for more profitable alcohol, rumrunners soon moved on to smuggling Canadian whiskey, French champagne and English gin to major cities like New York and Boston, where prices were high. Given its location and seafaring expertise, the mariners of P-Town and the entire coast of Mass Bay were well positioned to take advantage of this activity.

The population was bolstered by a number of Portuguese sailors, many of whom were from the Azores, who came to live in Provincetown after being hired to work on U.S. ships. By the 1890s, P-Town was booming and began to develop a resident population of writers and artists, as well as a summer tourist industry. After the 1898 *Portland* Gale severely damaged the town's fishing industry, members of the art community took over many of the abandoned buildings. By the early decades of the twentieth century, P-Town had acquired an international reputation for its artistic and literary output. It still had, however, a reputation among mariners for dangerous shoals, storms and bad luck.

During the Revolutionary War, the wreck of the *Somerset* brought joy to the hearts of Cape Codders when she met her fate on Peaked Hill Bars on the backside of P-Town on November 2, 1778. According to William Quinn in his book *Shipwrecks Around Cape Cod*, the *Somerset* was a sixty-four-ton frigate built in Chatham, England, and launched in 1748. She covered the landing of the British troops for the Battle of Bunker Hill in Charlestown and was a frequent visitor to P-Town. While there, Captain Curry annoyed the locals by appropriating fresh supplies for his ship and not paying. Instead, he would send his chaplain ashore on Sundays to preach to the locals, no doubt about the virtues of serving his cause. Henry Wadsworth Longfellow wrote about the ship in his poem "Paul Revere's Ride," using *Somerset* as a metaphor for the evil British:

> *Just as the moon rose over the bay,*
> *Where swinging wide at her mooring lay*
> *The Somerset, the British Man-o-War;*
> *A phantom ship, with each mast and spar.*
> *Across the moon like a prison bar,*
> *And a huge black hulk, that was magnified*
> *By its own reflection in the tide.*

In 1778, while she was pursuing a French merchant ship, she failed to clear the sand bar called Peaked Hill Bars and broke up, with fifty crewmembers drowning. A militia assembled, captured the captain and marched him to a

Boston prison. Locals removed items of value from the ship, such as cannons and timber and burned the hull. It then succumbed to the sand and was not seen again until 1973 when the ribs of the *Somerset* peaked above the sand, causing a stir among locals, tourists and historians.

Coastal towns around Mass Bay benefited from wrecks, gathering the timbers and materials that washed ashore and using them to build houses and other structures. As we will see with the *Forest Queen*, sometimes valuable cargo was recovered that made the lucky scavenger quite wealthy. There are always rumors in coastal areas and islands that the locals are "wreckers"— that is, they cause a ship to wreck so they can collect the booty. One technique called mooncussing involved waving a lighted lantern on shore in a way to look like a ship bobbing in the waves. If you were lucky, a ship full of valuable cargo would follow that light to your shore, thinking it was a ship heading to a good harbor. Other techniques involved placing the lantern on a pole to imitate a lighthouse. Whether this ever happened in Mass Bay or any area with a "wreckers" mark from the Isles of Shoals to the Isles of Scilly from Nantucket to the Padre and Mustang Islands is open for discussion.

The *Whydah* was the unlucky flagship of the pirate "Black Sam" Bellamy. Some legends recount that Bellamy wanted to visit his mistress, Maria Hallett, who lived near P-Town, while others blame the *Whydah*'s route on navigator error. In any case, at midnight on April 26, 1717, she sailed into a violent storm and was driven onto the shoals at Wellfleet in what is now Marconi Beach on the backside of the Cape, about ten miles south of where the *Somerset* grounded. She quickly sank, taking Bellamy and the majority of his crew with it. By morning, 102 pirate corpses were washed up on the shoreline and hundreds of mooncussers began plundering the remains. One of the two surviving members of Bellamy's crew, Thomas Davis, testified in his subsequent trial that "in a quarter of an hour after the ship struck, the Mainmast was carried by the board, and in the Morning she was beat to pieces." Apparently, Maria, pregnant with Bellamy's child, died alone after the wreck but still walks the beaches as the "Ghost of Cape Cod." The wreck of the *Whydah* was rediscovered in 1984 by underwater explorer Barry Clifford, who relied heavily on a 1717 map of the wreck's location, and has been the site of extensive underwater archaeology. Many of the two hundred thousand or so artifacts recovered are housed in the *Whydah* Museum in P-Town.

Built in 1870, the 1,586-ton, 253-foot, three-masted British coal ship *Jason* was one unlucky ship. In February 1892, she collided with the steamer *Trilawie* while en route to Zanzibar. After being repaired and on her way, a

Bad-luck ship *Jason* at anchor. *Courtesy Truro Historical Society.*

crewman was washed overboard while rounding the Cape of Good Hope in a gale. She eventually made it to Zanzibar and discharged her cargo and set out for Calcutta, where they loaded ten thousand heavy bales of jute, a coarse fiber similar to cotton that can be spun into strong thread. While loading, one of the crewmembers fell overboard and drowned. Soon after the ship set off for Boston with its cargo, strong winds turned into a hurricane, which laid the ship on its beam-ends, broke the captain's leg and forced it into Mauritius for six months of repairs. Upon leaving the port with a new captain, another crewmember fell overboard and died. Shortly after that, they were forced to turn back to drop some of the jute cargo that had become wet and too swollen to fit in the hold of the ship. In the fall of 1893, the *Jason* finally departed again for America and soon found itself off the elbow of Cape Cod near the deadly Pollock Rip Shoals.

On December 5, 1893, the crew had been sailing on a lee shore—that is, being blown downwind onto the shore—and began to prepare lifeboats for the inevitable wreck. As the ship ran up the coast toward the spot of its eventual wreck, it was under the surveillance of every lifesaving station it passed. First reported off Orleans station, it passed Nauset Beach and the Pamet River Lifesaving Station. It finally hit a rock, ran aground and broke in half on a beach a half mile north of the Pamet River Station, in between where the *Whydah* and *Somerset* had wrecked, on what is now called Ballston Beach in Truro. The Pamet River Station crew rushed out to aid the vessel; unfortunately, most of her twenty-seven sailors had

Depiction of how the *Jason* wrecked half a mile north of the Pamet River Lifesaving Station in Truro in 1893. *Michelle Garcia, illustrator.*

already perished. The sole survivor, a boy named Samuel Evans, was swept overboard by the storm, clutched onto a floating bale of jute and was picked up on shore. Confirming the supposed bad luck that was carried by the *Jason*, Samuel Evans fell from his bunk during his very next voyage and was killed. Some believe that every sailor on the *Jason* was doomed from the day they departed, but Samuel Evans just received his fate later than the others. Many of the crewmembers that went down with the ship are buried in the Wellfleet Oak Dale Cemetery, where a monument was erected in 1976 honoring the twenty-seven unfortunate mariners.

The result of most wrecks is that the ship will sink to the bottom of the ocean, where she will remain, left to the enjoyment of wreck divers and fish. In the case of the submarine *S-4*, she started out underwater, surfaced, was wrecked, sank, resurfaced, repaired and put back in service. Not, however, before sadly losing her crew.

For three thousand years, man has sought advantage by going below the surface of the ocean, especially in wartime. The first published description for a submarine came from English innkeeper William Bourne in 1578. Bourne offered a clear description of why a ship floats—by displacing its

A half mile away the prow of the wreck Jason, with its white figurehead, rose clean out of the water, standing where she struck the night of the 5th of December, nearly two years ago. The iron schooner broke clean in two that night with the first shock, and the waves rushed over her stern, which sank like lead into the sand. Twenty-seven men went down with it, and next morning twenty-six dead bodies lay upon the shore in among the scattered bales of jute that had formed the cargo. But the twenty-seventh, reaching the shore alive, managed to clutch hold of one of the bales of the floating cargo and kept his footing. He was a young fellow, a 'prentice lad out of an English rectory, and he was very nearly exhausted with the struggle, but he staggered on along the sand through the storm until he met the squad of the life-saving crew coming to give help where there was only one man left to need it, and catching at the first man he cried out to know if he was safe. When they told him that he was, he fell down in a faint, and was carried to the station like a log. The letter his father wrote in gratitude for their care of him is kept among the records of the station, and it is one of the few pleasant things to remember about the most terrible wreck that had ever lain on the dangerous Truro coast.

Newspaper article on the wreck of the *Jason* in 1893.

weight of water—and then described how it could sink and refloat: "It is possible to make a Ship or Boate that may goe under the water unto the bottome, and so to come up again at your pleasure. If any magnitude of body that is in the water...having alwaies but one weight, may be made bigger or lesser, then it Shall swimme when you would, and sinke when you list."

Decrease the volume to make the boat denser than the water it displaces, and it will sink. Make it less dense by increasing the volume, and it will rise. Using this principle, the first successful submarine was built in 1620 and was propelled by oars. The first military submarine was the *Turtle*, a hand-powered, egg-shaped device that accommodated a single man, built in 1776. In 1814, during the War of 1812, a submarine was used in an unsuccessful attack on a British warship stationed in New London Harbor. Subs have been used in every war since, from the American Civil War to the Russo-Japanese War to World War I, when they started to have significant impact, to World War II and into the present. They have also operated extensively in and around the waters of Mass Bay.

Late in the morning of July 21, 1918, a periscope broke the surface off the backside of P-Town near Nauset Beach. It was from *U-156*, a large German Imperial Navy submarine. In short order, the sub shelled and sank the 138-foot tug *Perth Amboy* and the four barges she was towing, then slipped back into the deep. Hundreds of people on the shore witnessed the attack; local newspapers demanded investigation as to why the navy base close by in Chatham did not respond. Most of the crew from the air station was in P-Town that morning for a friendly baseball game. Luckily, no one died on the tug and barges from the attack, though there were several injuries. Nine years later, the sub *S-4* nearly a mile off Wood End Light was not so lucky.

The USS *S-4*, an 876-ton S-3 class submarine, was built by the Portsmouth Navy Yard, located in Kittery, Maine, in 1919. She served for eight years in the Gulf of Mexico, Philippines, Panama, Hawaii and then off the coast of New England beginning in the spring of 1927.

Named after Civil War admiral Hiram Paulding, the USS *Paulding*, a 293-foot, 742-ton destroyer, was built at Bath, Maine, in 1910. She operated with the Atlantic Fleet's torpedo force, mainly along the East Coast, though during World War One, operated off the British Isles doing anti-submarine patrol and escort duty in the U-boat infested waters. In 1924, renamed USCGC *Paulding*, she ran rum patrol to enforce the prohibition against alcoholic beverages.

Rum patrol was an operation of the Coast Guard to interdict liquor-smuggling rumrunners to enforce Prohibition in American waters, especially in Mass Bay, where rumrunning was a profitable and popular endeavor. To deal with this problem, twenty-five destroyers like the *Paulding* were transferred from the U.S. Navy to the Coast Guard. These were by far the largest and most sophisticated vessels ever operated by the Coast Guard, and trained personnel were hard to find. As a result, Congress authorized hundreds of new enlistees; Coast Guard destroyers were generally made up of these inexperienced crews.

On December 17, 1927, while conducting submerged trials off Provincetown, the *S-4* was rammed by the *Paulding*. Holed in the starboard side, just forward of her deck gun, the submarine sank immediately. *Paulding* stopped and lowered lifeboats but found only a small amount of oil and air bubbles. As the submarine sank to the bottom, 110 feet below, all of the officers and men on the *S-4* were able to reach unflooded compartments. However, the majority, who had gone aft, soon drowned as those areas flooded. In her forward torpedo room, six men remained dry and alive. In extremely cold water and tangled wreckage, navy divers worked desperately to rescue them. The six men exchanged a series of signals with divers by tapping on the hull. As the trapped men used the last available oxygen in the sub, a diver placed his helmeted ear to the side of the vessel and received this Morse-coded message: "Is … there … any … hope?" Sadly, there was no reason for hope, and the remaining six men perished, for a total of forty lost.

Miles Henslow, in his book *Fifty Great Disasters that Shocked the World*, described the event this way:

Depiction of the collision between USCGC *Paulding* and submarine *S-4*. *Michelle Garcia, illustrator.*

The surface of the ocean was clear from horizon to horizon, and to all intents and purposes there was no need for an attending ship to hoist the "Submarine Flag"—an indication that a boat is under water. Surface trials were carried out according to plan, the crew soon accustomed themselves to the feel of the boat, and the order was given to dive. Hatches were closed, men took up diving stations, and the tanks were flooded; diesel engines stopped, and with her propellers running from power stored in her giant batteries, S-4 sank slowly into the waves. The land was as quiet as it was those centuries before, when the Pilgrim Fathers first reached the shore; and the bay and the sea was as empty and unbroken as it had been that day when the pioneers' white sails first cut across the horizon.

Presently, all underwater trials satisfactorily completed, the tanks would be blown; bubbles would rise from the depths as the water ballast was forced from the hollow sides and bottom; a feather of foam would appear as the submarine's eye protruded, followed rapidly, foot by foot, by the sleek grey sides of the conning tower.

Steaming along at an easy 18 knots, the Paulding drew nearer and nearer to Provincetown Harbor. Her helmsman, roving eyes automatically on the water ahead, saw a long stick-like object projecting from the waves, almost under her bows—just the type of stick which many of the local fishermen used to mark their nets. Instinctively he swung the helm over, wishing to avoid any obstructions. But, even as he swung the wheel, a dark shadow appeared at the base of the stick. Almost under the bows of the ship, rising in a froth of bubbles, was the glint of metal. In a few split seconds the innocent "stick" had reared up nearly twenty feet. A lightning order for "Full speed and full rudder" was of no avail.

Nothing on this earth could have saved what followed. By the most tragic of coincidences, all unknown to each other, the captains of those two boats had set their courses so that they crossed. Rising from the depths, unseen, unexpected, the S-4 broke surface a bare few feet from Paulding's sharp bows. There was a grinding crash, and a shriek of tortured steel. Paulding hesitated, shivering from stem to stern under the impact.

It was all over so quickly that S-4 had disappeared before all those on board Paulding knew the cause of the shock. A few seconds previously the surface of the sea had been a wide expanse of waves, chopping and rolling without interruption, from horizon to coast. Without the slightest warning hint of her presence, S-4 appeared from nowhere, as though mysteriously attracted to the spot. Followed a ghastly crash and a shock which hurled

USCGC *Paulding* in drydock after the collision.

This page: Submarine *S-4* in drydock after being refloated and towed to Boston Navy Yard. Note the extensive damage.

men from their feet, and once more the surface of the sea was unbroken save by waves. Even as the Paulding was slowed and stopped, great bubbles rose and burst by her side. A grim and tell-tale patch of oil appeared and spread. Boats were lowered at once, ready to pick up any S-4 men who might have survived, but not a trace of wreckage or a sign of life was seen; and Paulding, herself in a sinking condition, was obliged to make for the shore at all speed, otherwise she might well have followed the submarine to the bottom of the ocean. A buoy was hastily dropped to mark the scene of the tragedy, and her captain rang the engines "Full Ahead," even while the radio crackled out its terrible message:

"Rammed and apparently sank S-4 at 15.37 (3.37 p.m.) off Wood End Coastguard Station. Boats searching for survivors. Paulding Provincetown Harbor. Lower hold filled. Will probably have to beach her."

During the first three months of 1928, divers and other salvage personnel were able to raise the sunken *S-4* and tow her to the Boston Navy Yard, where she was dry-docked and repaired. She returned to active duty in October as a submarine rescue and salvage test ship. The dive rescue tests, research and training on the *S-4* both during and after her wreck helped develop equipment such as the rescue bell and techniques that bore fruit a decade later when thirty-three men were brought up alive from the sunken submarine *Squalus*. Also built at the Portsmouth Navy Yard, the *Squalus* was launched in 1939 and sunk during trials that same year near the Isles of Shoals. The *Paulding* was taken to dry dock, repaired and returned to service. An inquiry in to the sinking of *S-4* absolved her of all blame.

CHAPTER 7

PINTHIS-FAIRFAX

BUOY 4 HUMAROCK

42° 9.18N
70° 33.48W

The *Mayflower* set sail from England on September 6, 1620, filled with Pilgrims and, after a grueling sixty-six-day journey marked by disease, which claimed two lives, dropped anchor inside Provincetown. The settlers, upon initially setting anchor, explored the snow-covered area and discovered a seemingly empty Native American village. Across the dunes from where the *Jason* grounded, the curious settlers dug up some artificially made mounds, some of which stored corn while others were burial sites. They moved down the coast to what is now Eastham and explored Cape Cod for several weeks and, depending on what historian you read, looting and stealing, or trading and borrowing, for the food they needed. Finding Provincetown unsuitable for farming and safe habitation, the *Mayflower* weighed anchor and crossed Cape Cod Bay to Plymouth in December 1620.

As we proceed along our journey and head across the bay, as the Pilgrims did, we come upon the largest town by area in the state, at 134 square miles, about a fifth the size of Mass Bay. Throughout the nineteenth century, Plymouth thrived as a center of fishing and shipping and once held the world's largest rope making company, the Plymouth Cordage Company. Though tricky to navigate owing to the many shoals and long channel, Plymouth continues to be an active port; however, its major industry is now tourism. As one of the country's first settlements, Plymouth has become part of American mythology, particularly those relating to Plymouth Rock, the Pilgrims and the First Thanksgiving.

In December 1778, one month after the British ship *Somerset* went down on the backside of P-Town, the one-hundred-foot American brigantine *General Arnold* headed out of Nantasket Roads, Boston Harbor. Skippered by James Magee, an Irish-born American patriot, the *Arnold* carried twenty guns, a detachment of marines and cargo for the American troops fighting the British to the south. As the ship sailed out, accompanied by a privateer *Revenge*, the wind picked up and quickly turned into a nor'easter. Magee felt his ship would weather the storm better in Plymouth Harbor behind the headland of Gurnet Point, but the *Arnold*'s anchors would not hold and she began to drift into the long harbor. Attempts to add weight and stability failed, and with the ship bucking, her anchors soon parted. She sailed backward deeper into the harbor, grounding on a sand flat, not far from where the *Mayflower* found Plymouth Rock 158 years earlier. Efforts to lighten ship and get off the bar failed, and the *Arnold* stranded.

Local mariners quickly rowed out in dories to investigate but failed to get close enough to the *Arnold* and returned to port. They then proceeded to build a mile-long ice and snow road out to the ship as the nor'easter continued to build and temperatures drop. To keep from freezing to death, Magee forced his crew to stay awake and walk. After the third night of the wreck, the road was completed and the rescuers passed over the ice causeway to the ship. One of the first to board, Doctor Thatcher described it this way:

> *It was a scene unutterably awful and distressing. The ship was sunk ten feet in the sand; the waves had been for about 36 hours sweeping the main deck, and even here they were obliged to pile together dead bodies to make room for the living. Seventy bodies, frozen into all imaginable postures, were strewn over the deck or attached to shrouds and spars; about thirty exhibited signs of life, but were unconscious whether in life or death. The bodies remained in the posture in which they died, the features dreadfully distorted. Some were erect, some bending forward, some sitting with the head resting on the knee, and some with both arms extended, clinging to spars or some parts of the vessel.*

When local minister Chandler Robbins came to the courthouse to perform funeral services for the eighty-one deceased, the horror caused him to faint. A mass grave was dug at Plymouth's Burial Hill for sixty-six men, some frozen together with other men as they had tried in vain to stay alive. Captain Magee didn't suffer frostbite, though he was anguished for the rest of his life, which ended in 1801; he was buried with his crew on Burial Hill.

His one regret was his decision to turn in to Plymouth Harbor to escape the brunt of the storm, especially since the *Revenge* rode out the storm out to sea. In the 1970s, the skeletal remains of a shipwreck emerged from the waters of White Flat; archaeologists and historians researched the remains and concluded that it was the wreck of the *General Arnold*.

As you leave Plymouth and head north, you will pass the spot where, according to Robert Ellis Cahill, scuba diver Jim Baldi discovered the find of the century in the early 1980s: a French merchant ship that wrecked off Marshfield in a storm in 1616, well before the *Mayflower* arrived. As we have seen before, the location of this wreck was first noted by fishermen as they pulled up parts of the ship in their nets. Part of a conquistador's helmet was netted from the depths off Marshfield in the early 1900s, and a large iron claw used as a lantern on ancient vessels was pulled up in the same area in 1944. By accident, a lobsterman pulled up a large encrusted bronze shield off Brant Rock in 1952. It was covered with thick layers of sea growth, but once cleaned, the face of a shield revealed carvings of charging horses and dueling warriors.

According to Cahill, archeologists who saw the shield believe it may be Phoenician, Roman or possibly Celtic. Diving in the area where these artifacts were pulled up, Baldi has uncovered a pewter spoon, cannonballs, doughnut-shaped pullies and old timbers sticking out of the bottom of the sea floor. Without more research, including raising the ship from the deep, it is hard to know how old these artifacts are. It is also possible these artifacts did not come from a Phoenician vessel of ancient times but could have been dropped overboard or sunk with a fairly modern ship, perhaps one that was returning from Europe with artifacts destined for a museum or private collector.

Scuba divers continue to scour the floor of Mass Bay for interesting artifacts and treasure. Breaking the important "buddy rule," some of these divers dive alone, preferring to keep any wrecks and artifacts they discover to themselves; others join one of the many excellent dive clubs around Mass Bay. In any case, when a wreck is discovered, a range of specific rules apply, from prohibiting disruption and removal of any artifacts, as with the *Portland*, to "exempting" it to some degree, as with the *Chester A. Poling*, so that wreck divers can enjoy exploring it and pulling up artifacts. Established in 1973, the Massachusetts Board of Underwater Archaeological Resources is charged with managing Mass Bay's underwater heritage and promoting and protecting the public's interests in these resources for recreational, economic, environmental and historical purposes. Led by Victor Mastone, director of the board, several key specific rules for divers are as follows:

No person may remove, displace, damage or destroy any underwater archaeological resource except in conformity with permits issued by the Board. The three types of permits are established for the non-destructive inspection and identification of underwater archaeological resources and are characterized by minimum site disturbance; to uncover and/or remove underwater archaeological resources through the use of disruptive investigation techniques; and for environmental review, public planning, and scientific research projects.

To deal with certain types of artifact discoveries, the Board's regulations provide an exemption from the permit process for isolated finds and exempted sites. The purpose in creating an exempted shipwreck site is to preserve such sites for the continued enjoyment of the recreational diving community. Recreational diving activities, including casual artifact collection, on exempted shipwreck sites does not require a permit from the Board. However, any major disruption of the site is prohibited.

The Board may establish underwater archaeological preserves. The purpose of underwater archaeological preserves is to recognize and protect those resources of substantial archaeological and/or historical value. While access for recreational, scientific and historical purposes is guaranteed, collecting will not be allowed except for scientific or historical purposes, and the artifacts remain the permanent property of the Commonwealth.

Working hand and hand with the Massachusetts Board of Underwater Archaeological Resources, Bill Carter was one of the most accomplished divers in Mass Bay for the past fifty years. As I stated in the introduction, he dove many wrecks such as the *Albert Gallatin* off Manchester, *City of Salisbury* near Graves Light, *Delaware* off Minot's Ledge, *Forest Queen* off Scituate, *Chester A. Poling* off Gloucester and, his favorite, the *Pinthis* off Humarock. A decade ago, with Carter well into his seventies, he stopped diving and shifted his focus to sharing his experiences. He was instrumental in establishing some of the exhibits at the Maritime and Irish Mossing Museum in Scituate, Massachusetts. The pride of Bill's collection is the whistle from the tanker *Pinthis*.

There are many questions regarding the collision of the *Pinthis* and the *Fairfax* on June 10, 1930, six miles east of Scituate's Humarock Beach. Built in 1919, the steel coastal tanker *Pinthis* was a typical diesel vessel of the day. Following departure from Fall River, Massachusetts, with twelve thousand barrels of oil, the *Pinthis* collided in fog with the steamer *Fairfax*, sustaining a mortal blow. It blew up and, in less than twenty minutes, capsized and sank, taking all nineteen crewmembers to the deep. Coupled with those that died

Pinthis dockside, circa 1928.

on the *Fairfax*, fifty-one people lost their lives from this tragedy—though this exact number is in dispute. This is the basic story, but exactly what happened may never be fully known. Other than the survivors on the *Fairfax*, no one saw the *Pinthis* sink or the terrified passengers of the *Fairfax* leap into the sea to escape the flames. Apparently both ships had experienced crews and navigation aids, so why did they collide? Why wasn't the Coast Guard, or any vessel in the area, called sooner? The investigation that followed the collision did not answer many of these questions. We do know for certain that this was the worst maritime wreck Scituate and Marshfield have experienced.

Not a pretty ship, the steel-hulled coastal tanker *Pinthis* was built in Newburg, New York. She was 206 feet long, had a 35-foot beam and displaced 1,111 gross tons. She was powered by a four-cylinder, five-hundred-horsepower, Bolinder diesel engine with a cruising speed of nine knots. She was originally owned by Sugar Products Company and transported molasses from the Caribbean to the United States. At the time of the collision, the tanker was owned by Lake Tankers and leased to Shell Oil Company. This type of tanker was used in the coastal trade and didn't possess the range of equipment and aids found on larger vessels, such as radios and modern navigation equipment. Operating close to shore, she used dead reckoning. The steam whistle—used to alert other ships in poor visibility and announce ship's turns—recovered and cleaned up by Bill Carter was unusually large for this size ship. It was taken by Captain Albert Jones from a large tanker he spotted aground in Newport, Rhode Island, in 1924 and put aboard the *Pinthis* when he assumed command. For six years, Jones, a graduate of the Massachusetts Maritime Academy, had been master. At age thirty-six, he was the youngest captain on the east coast. He was a dedicated family man who refused larger commands overseas because he did not want to be away from his wife and daughter for too long.

Albert Jones, captain of the *Pinthis*.

The *Fairfax* was placed in service in 1926 by the Merchant & Miners Transportation Company of Baltimore. She was 363 feet long, grossed 5,600 tons and could carry 285 passengers. Like other ships of this type, she also carried freight, which was an important source of revenue. To entertain passengers, she had a dance hall, music room and social hall. Half the staterooms had a private bath. During the summer, the *Fairfax* ran from Boston to Norfolk; in the winter, she ran from Baltimore to ports in Florida. The captain of the *Fairfax* was Archie H. Brooks. He had extensive sea experience and was conscientious, spending the two weeks prior to the collision as a pilot on the Cape Cod Canal to learn the finer details. Like Captain Jones of the *Pinthis*, he had an unrestricted license. At forty, he was a stocky man with a distinctive southern drawl.

According to Keatts, the *Pinthis* had an uneventful passage through Cape Cod Canal and into Cape Cod Bay at 5:00 p.m. on the tenth of June. As she headed north, the fog was thickening, and as dusk settled, it became even denser. The captain ordered the fog signal sounded every minute. Captain Jones was unaware of the fast approach of the passenger liner *Fairfax* heading south with seventy-six passengers and a crew of eighty. Just after 7:00 p.m. and cruising over eleven knots, a ship suddenly appeared off the starboard

Fairfax underway. *Courtesy Bill Carter.*

Fairfax drydock.
Courtesy Bill Carter.

Depiction of *Fairfax-Pinthis* collision on June 10, 1930, as reported by *Fairfax* survivors. *Michelle Garcia, illustrator.*

After the collision, the surface continued to burn for twenty-four hours.

bow blowing her whistle. The helmsman of the *Fairfax* put the helm hard over and reversed the engines. However, thirty seconds after sighting, the momentum of the big ship caused it to slice into the *Pinthis*. Immediately, the *Pinthis* burst into flames, sending blazing oil and gasoline into the air, raining fire down on both ships. According to reports, the *Pinthis* attached to the *Fairfax* and started to sink immediately. The *Fairfax* continued to back down but was unable to decouple until the *Pinthis* fell below the waves and started to turn over.

With the forward decks on fire, Captain Brooks quickly maneuvered the ship into the lee, to prevent the spread of the fire aft. The crew and passengers, including several U.S. Navy seamen, started battling the flames. Unfortunately, several passengers perished in the flames; others panicked and jumped into the sea with or without lifejackets. Although the *Pinthis* had sunk, oil and gasoline continued to escape her holds, fanning a growing fire on the surface that lasted for several days. Many who jumped in were burned to death by these flames. The fires aboard the liner were eventually

Article from the *Boston Evening Globe* on June 11, 1930, one day after the *Fairfax-Pinthis* collision.

Article from the *Boston Evening Post* on June 12, 1930, two days after the *Fairfax-Pinthis* collision.

extinguished by the combined efforts of the crew and passengers and limped back to port under her own power. Although Brooks requested help removing passengers from his sister ship *Gloucester*, it is unclear when he asked for this help. It is also unclear if Brooks alerted the Coast Guard or any other lifesaving service with an SOS in a timely fashion and with accurate information. In any event, the Coast Guard did not respond for twenty-four hours, during which time, people all along the South Shore watched the ocean burn.

As with any wreck, especially when people die, there is an investigation, in public, along the docks and in the courts. For the public, this story had it all: death, fire, survival, heroism, blame, mystery and coverup. The newspapers interviewed survivors, families of those killed, the owner—anyone associated—and ran sensational stories for months. The *Quincy Evening News* on June 12 carried a story under the headline "Quincy Couple Claim Laxity On Death Ship." The story quoted a passenger,

> *I didn't see a single ship's officer during the first hour after the ship hit. Then they seemed to be running around uselessly. The marines and the gobs organized a fire fighting force and with the aid of the men passengers and some of the crew we finally got the fire out after a three hour fight. Then I went up above and found three officers whispering together. One was the captain. I said "see here, if I was captain of this ship I'd go below and talk to the passengers and calm them." They didn't know whether we are going to float or go down in five minutes. A lot of the women are hysterical. They didn't say a word, just walked away and the captain didn't give a word of any kind to the passengers.*

Dave Ball wrote the definitive account of the collision and subsequent investigation in his book *Night of Terror at Buoy Number Four*. The title comes from the navigation aid Buoy Four near where the ships collided; Buoy Four has since been move east a half mile and renamed RW "H." According to Ball, there were many unanswered questions, and soon the politicians joined the fray, saying if they didn't get answers, they would start their own investigations. The Department of Commerce's Steamboat Inspection Service was the agency responsible for conducting the federal inquiry. Hearings began on June 12 at the Appraisers Building in Boston, led by local inspectors Charles Lyons and John Stewart. Lyon, in fact, started his own investigation right away, meeting the *Fairfax* as soon as she docked. After talking with the ship's officers, Lyons told the press the ship's officers were "gambling with lives out there." Lyons went on to say, "I asked Captain Brooks why he did not send for a Coast Guard ship when he ascertained how many were injured and to what extent. He replied he thought they were giving the burned and injured the best treatment possible." Cutting to the chase, Lyons continued,

> *A Coast Guard boat could have found the Fairfax, transferred the injured and would have had them in a hospital at 11 pm at the latest. The failure to call the Coast Guard for these two reasons—the possibility of rescuing those in the water and to get the injured in as fast as possible—is what I would call gross negligence of the worst sort. The whole matter of loss of life and other happenings along that line—in other words what transpired after the collision—simmers down to the failure of Brooks to send an SOS. He had no idea what would happen and had no right to gamble with those lives. Although it will all be thrashed out today at the inquiry, the contents of the Brooks log show that according to the rules of the sea, the Fairfax should have been stopped and reversed. He heard a whistle in the fog and simply reduced speed. He says he heard the whistle on his starboard and even under clear weather conditions he should be on the watch for that ship to cross his bow.*

The purpose of the inquiry was to sort out all the details of the collision and determine if any of the *Fairfax* officers were culpable. They would examine four basic questions, according to Ball:

1. *Which ship was responsible for the crash?*
2. *Did the Fairfax properly radio requests for help?*

3. Was there an adequate search conducted for victims?
4. Was everything possible done for the injured passengers?

The first witness to testify was Captain Brooks, and the question of the *Fairfax*'s speed was explored. Brooks states that full speed for his ship was 13.5 knots and that he ran it at half speed after leaving the pier and continued at half speed, slowing a couple times to listen for buoys and ships. However, simple mathematics proved otherwise. The total distance from Boston to Buoy Four is twenty-seven miles. Obviously, the *Fairfax* proceeded slowly through the harbor so the ship couldn't have been steaming at half speed from the lightship Lyon interrupted Brook's testimony and said, "Your log book show that you were going 11.2 knots instead of half speed. Is that a moderate speed in fog, captain?" Brooks nodded yes. Lyons then asked what was a low speed for the ship, and the captain said it was 6.76 knots. Finally, Brook said he considered moderate speed to be between 10–11 knots. Lyons countered by saying, "Well then captain, there doesn't seem to be much difference between full and moderate speed." It seemed obvious the *Fairfax* was going too fast for the dense fog they faced on the tenth.

The officers of the *Fairfax* followed Brooks and confirmed that there was no panic on the ship, the fire was out in less than half an hour and everything possible was done to reduce the danger to the passengers. Third Officer Powell detailed how he conducted the two-hour search for victims in the water. Powell also stated he thought the *Pinthis* had the right of way at the time of the collision, a seemingly important admission that was not followed up.

Radio operator J. Wesley Geweken was the next witness, and he told them he sent an SOS eight or ten times before the fire forced him out of the radio room. Lyons then asked him, "What is your theory when the Navy, the Coast Guard, and a score of other shore stations were listening anxiously because of the fog, why they didn't hear your SOS?" Geweken responded, "The antenna must have been down when I sent it." The last question was one of the most important of the inquiry and one that many reporters had waited two days to hear. Lyons asked Geweken what message he received from the USCG cutter *Tampa*. He responded, "He called and asked if everything was all right. I answered, yes, we are waiting for the *Gloucester* to take off our passengers. They gave no name when they asked, but they said they were the Coast Guard cutter." Lyon followed up, "You said everything was all right, when a number of people burned, two of them so badly burned they died afterward?" Geweken replied, "Yes; everything was all right, compared to what it had been."

During the second day of testimony, Captain Frederic Gower, manager of the company that operated the *Pinthis* gave startling testimony. According to Gower, there was not a burn, bruise of blemish on Captain Jones, Second Mate Charles Weisser or seaman Corboy, raising the question about whether or not all on the *Pinthis* burned to death or drowned. The Cape Cod pilot was also quizzed about the length of a proper search, which he thought would be forty-eight hours, not the two-hour search actually conducted.

The commander of the Coast Guard vessel *Tampa* and her radio operator also testified. Commander Stanley Parker stated that he was twenty-three miles from the *Pinthis* and could have reached her in less than an hour. The radioman stated he heard no SOS from the *Fairfax*. He testified the Nahant Coast Guard Station asked, "What is disposition of the crew? What is the name of the tanker sunk? At what time was it sunk?" The *Fairfax* unbelievably radioed back a brief message, "Tanker sunk at 7:05, June 10. Do not know name of tanker. None of crew saved."

After considering all the testimony at the Steamboat Inspection Service hearing in Boston, the inspectors determined there was sufficient evidence to put Captain Brooks on trial. The trial opened on August 12, 1930, in Norfolk, Virginia, a place southerner Brooks probably found friendlier than Boston. He faced many charges, including excessive speed in fog, lack of skill and negligence. Brook again pleaded not guilty; twenty-seven witnesses testified, corroborating much of what was heard earlier. On August 27, the steamboat inspectors announced they had acquitted Captain Brooks of all charges determining:

1. *Fairfax searched the waters for the victims for a sufficient distance and time.*
2. *Captain Brooks used prudent but unsuccessful measure to avoid a collision.*
3. *Fairfax was making only three knots at the time of the collision.*
4. *Pinthis was making her maximum speed at the time of the collision.*
5. *No one on Fairfax heard the Pinthis sound any fog signals prior to colliding.*

The actions of the Coast Guard also came under fire after the disaster. The key question was why it took a full day to respond. After an investigation, the Coast Guard was exonerated, with the *Boston Post* providing this summary on June 18: "To attach any blame at all to any Coast Guard unit in connection with the disaster would be grossly unfair to the Coast Guard service. Whatever blame at all for the events that transpired in the wake of the disaster belong squarely upon the shoulders of those who neglected, refused, or failed to send out an SOS." The report squarely placed the blame on the *Fairfax* and the cause of the collision as "*Fairfax*'s excessive speed and other violations."

On July 29, 1930, Hubert Grove made the first successful dive on the *Pinthis*. Hired by the *Pinthis*'s insurance underwriters to survey the wreck, he found the ship in ninety-six feet of water, resting partially on her port side, in a general east-west orientation, bow to stern. He told reporters that he saw a hole on the port side but couldn't tell how big; there was no damage on the starboard side. The underwriters asked Grove to check the bridge telegraph to find out how fast it was going when disaster struck. The speed indicator was set at half speed, giving further proof that Captain Jones was proceeding prudently. Eerily, Grove also found several bodies tangled in lines inside the bridge. According to Keatts, the *Pinthis* capsized as she sank and is now keel up in sand and gravel. This discrepancy between Keatts and Grove is perhaps explained by the settling of the hull over time.

Today it is a popular dive spot not only for experienced diver seeking artifacts but also new divers seeking deep-water training. I dove on it five years ago, found it interesting, with visibility around ten feet and cold; the hull is collapsing on the seafloor. After years of exploring the wreck, Bill Carter and Tom Mulloy have discovered many clues to the final moments of the *Pinthis*. One puzzling question for the investigator at the hearing in 1930 was the type of damage to the *Pinthis*'s bow. Witnesses told inspectors the *Fairfax* struck the *Pinthis* on her port bow; yet, there were only scratches there, while the *Fairfax*'s starboard bow had a huge jagged hole. Grove, the diver who reached the wreck in 1930, thought he saw a hole on the port side, but it was difficult to confirm, given that the ship was lying on that side. Today, divers can see the entire hull because it has shifted upside down, and there is clearly no hole on the port bow. Carter and Mulloy point to the type of damage that can still be seen on the *Pinthis*: a sharp crease in the bottom of the starboard side near the propeller, a crushed skeg and a gaping hole in the engine room. This indicates that perhaps the *Pinthis* turned sharply away from the *Fairfax* when it saw it come out of the fog but failed to get out of the way fast enough. The starboard bow of the bigger vessel ran up and was punctured by the stern of the tanker, possibly even turning the Pinthis over, creasing the hull and crushing its skeg.

CHAPTER 8

FOREST QUEEN

THIRD CLIFF

42 ° 11.05N
70 ° 43.06W

Scituate sits the South Shore, midway between where the *City of Salisbury* went down in Boston Harbor and where the *General Arnold* froze in Plymouth. The town was settled about 1627 by a group from Plymouth, Massachusetts, and immigrants from the County of Kent, England. Incorporated in 1636, the name Scituate is derived from Satuit, a Wampanoag term for the cold brook that runs to the inner harbor of the town. Twelve homes and a sawmill were destroyed in King Philip's War in 1676. In 1717, the western portion of the original grant was separated and incorporated as the town of Hanover, and in 1788, a section of the town was ceded to Marshfield. In 1849, another western section became the town of South Scituate, which later changed its name to Norwell.

Traditionally, fishing was a significant part of the local economy, as was the Irish Mossing industry introduced in the nineteenth century. A small fishing fleet is still based in Scituate Harbor, although today the town is mostly residential. As we discussed in Chapter Two on the *Etrusco*, Scituate Light was erected in 1810 on the northern edge of Scituate Harbor. During the War of 1812, a British naval raiding party was deterred by the two daughters of the lighthouse keeper playing a fife and drum; they became known as the "Army of Two." In Chapter Six, we discussed the *Shannon-Chesapeake* battle of 1813, witnessed by many Scituate residents. Minot's Ledge Lighthouse stands approximately one mile east of Scituate Neck and Cohasset Harbor. Numerous wrecks have happened on these ledges, including the *St. John* discussed in Chapter Three and the *Delaware*, one of the casualties of the fierce *Portland* Gale of 1898.

The town is not contiguous; Humarock is a part of Scituate, which can only be reached from Marshfield. The latter was formerly connected to the town, but that connection was lost when the mouth of the North River shifted northward as a result of the *Portland* Gale of 1898. The town's shore varies, with the south along the mouth of the North River surrounded by salt marshes, the middle around Scituate Harbor being sandy and the coast of Scituate Neck at Minot in the north exhibiting exposed granite bedrock. The town is predominantly of European descent, mostly Irish, and was noted to be the most Irish town in the United States during the last census. Scituate reminded the Irish that settled here in the nineteenth century so much of their homeland that the town was often referred to as the "Irish Riviera."

Two important geographical features of the town have played a major role in wrecks along Mass Bay: the northeast-facing coastline and the cliffs. Four cliffs or drumlins highlight the coastline from First Cliff at the entrance to the harbor south to Fourth Cliff in Humarock, which we have learned was separated from Third Cliff by the *Portland* Gale. A drumlin, from the Irish word *droimnín*, meaning "little ridge," is an elongated hill in the shape of an inverted spoon or half-buried egg formed by glacial ice acting on underlying unconsolidated till or glacial debris. Historically, large rocks rim

Third Cliff in Scituate as it would have looked in 1853. It has since been ringed with a granite seawall.

Depiction of the *Forest Queen* underway. *Michelle Garcia, illustrator.*

the cliffs and extend into the ocean; in between each of these cliffs are rocky beaches. The coastline generally faces northeast, which means ships and debris under a severe nor'easter, aided by a flood tide, will be pushed onto the Scituate coastline. We saw this with the *Etrusco* in 1956, the *Columbia* and *Delaware* in 1898 and the unknown ship that ran aground on Egypt Beach in 1844 whose crew rests in a mass grave behind the Congregational Church. We also see it with one of the most fascinating wrecks on the South Shore, the *Forest Queen*, which wrecked in 1851.

In 1849, Rufus Paige & Son, of Hollowell, Maine, and Atkins & Company, of New York, called for the construction of a sailing vessel with the intention of plying the China Trade. Southards shipyard was contracted and began construction of a fully rigged three-masted ship. The Southards for three generations were the most prominent builders of ships in Richmond, Maine, though I have found documentation that the *Forest Queen* may have been built in Bath, Maine. Launched in late 1849 and home ported in New York, the *Forest Queen* had a length of 158 feet, a 35-foot beam, 886 tons and drew 18 feet. Compared to clipper ships with very light burdens, such as the *Baltimore Clipper* at 200 tons, this ship carried more cargo but was slower. On June 15, 1850, the *Forest Queen* set out of New York for its first journey to the Far East. Ports of call during this three-year voyage included China, India, the Philippines, Ireland, England and, finally, Boston. Little did the owners know that the ship would not again grace New York waters.

Three years later, the *Forest Queen* met its end on the shores of Peggotty Beach, off Third Cliff in Scituate. On the evening of February 28, 1853, the *Forest Queen*, with her crew, cargo and forty-five Irish immigrants picked up in Queenstown, Ireland, was only thirty miles from Boston when a fierce nor'easter with gale force winds and blinding snow forced the ship southwest of her intended course. Captain Olney Lovett and crew tried in vain to save the ship. He may have mistaken Scituate Light or Minot's Lightship for Boston Light and ordered a turn to port toward Third Cliff. He also may

have simply been at the mercy of another notorious winter gale, as so many ships have been. Either way, she grounded hard, terrifying the passengers and crew as the icy surf rocked the ship.

As a fairly new ship, the *Forest Queen* was still strong and intact as she grounded hard on the sand and rocks along the north shore of Third Cliff. However, as the seas mounted on the ice-covered ship, she turned broadside to the pounding waves. The passengers must have been terrified throughout the night as the surf rocked their ship and sent waves of freezing spray over them. Daybreak brought a calmer sea and

Olney Lovett, captain of the Forest Queen. *Courtesy Tom Mulloy.*

Depiction of the *Forest Queen* wreck on Third Cliff, February 28, 1853. *Michelle Garcia, illustrator.*

hope, as rescuers along the beach were busy setting up for the rescue. Led by Daniel Ward, who lived a stone's throw away from the wreck on Third Cliff, all were rescued safely, with the captain last to leave. Hope of refloating her was dashed when the storm regained its intensity.

With the ship broadside to the beach, there was little anyone could do to save it. The news of the shipwreck spread, with many gathering on the beach to retrieve cargo as it washed ashore. The *Forest Queen* had a large cargo of Chinese porcelain and silk, wine and gin, indigo and dyes, gold watches and personal items. As she was in shallow water, once the seas calmed, scavengers boarded her and removed her rigging for use on other ships; her planking and ribs to build and repair local homes. Daniel Ward salvaged the wreck for four years and, according to legend, used the proceeds from selling what he recovered to buy dories and start the Irish Mossing business, which thrived in Scituate until 1995. Proving that one man's wreck is another man's treasure, he also was able to buy a bigger home and move his family to First Cliff. It was rumored that the treasure Daniel Ward recovered was part of a twelve-ton cache of silver ingots used by the Chinese to pay for the opium the *Forest Queen* sold them.

The disaster was covered extensively. The *New York Herald* reported on March 4, 1853:

> *Ship Forest Queen of New York, from London for Boston, ashore in Scituate beach, has bilged and is full of water, mainmast and mizzen topmast gone. A quantity of cargo was washed ashore in a damaged state, but a large part has gone out to sea with the ebb tide. Vessel is breaking up and will be a total loss…Her cargo was a very valuable one, and is mostly insured at different offices in Boston.*

The New York Shipping and Commercial List reported two days later:

> *Ship Forest Queen of this port from London via Queenstown for Boston ran upon Scituate beach near third cliff on the 28th night, having mistaken Scituate Light for the lightship at Minot's Ledge. She lies broadside on, and it the weather proves favorable, will probably be set off, with little damage. Crew and passengers landed safely…*

Note that the reporter above referred to the Minot's Lightship, which was in place following the destruction of the nine-iron pile lighthouse in 1851. Note also his optimism that the ship would be refloated in good shape. Other reports detailed the difficult voyage of the *Forest Queen*: "She left the Downs December 19th and afterward experienced a series of gales which caused her cargo to shift and destroyed her spars, sails, etc, compelling her to put in to Queenstown, Ireland where she arrived January 3rd for repairs and set sail again on January 23rd." Several newspapers reported the captain was Captain Cooper; however, that seems incorrect. More credible data and personalized artifacts recovered from the wreck, including a bullhorn with Lovett's initials, indicate that the captain was Captain Olney Lovett.

Tom Mulloy has an uncanny eye for identifying old wrecks and artifacts that have blended through the centuries with the sand, rock and seaweed on the ocean floor. In 1991, he swam across a huge mass of fused debris underwater, about one hundred yards from Peggotty Beach. One chunk had broken off, so Mulloy hoisted it to the surface with the help of his dive buddies Debra Jackson, Rick Morse and Paul Figueiredo, cleaned it up and realized that he had discovered a seventy-three-pound ingot of what appeared to be pure silver, which if melted down would be worth about $4,000. Because of the chemical reactions that fuse metals in salt water, the wreckage resembles puddingstone, a conglomerate so impermeable that hammers and chisels barely make a dent. Subsequent processing of the concretions brought to the surface—not easy work—revealed many artifacts from Chinese porcelain, a captain's horn, a bottle of Lea Perrins Worcestershire sauce, champagne, another ingot and various pieces hardware and fittings. Further research revealed Mulloy had rediscovered the *Forest Queen*.

For the past two decades, Tom Mulloy, Hank Lynch and Debra Jackson have worked closely with the Massachusetts Division of Marine Archaeology and Director Victor Mastone to maintain a state permit and exclusive rights to excavate the *Forest Queen* site. With over four hundred dives on the wreck, they have cataloged and preserved artifacts for educational purposes, coordinating the *Forest Queen* history with local schools history curriculum and establishing an exhibit at the Scituate Maritime and Irish Mossing Museum. They have continued their research with well-constructed diagrams of the debris field, a diagram of the ship collapsing in the days following the wreck and an analysis of the Chinese marking on the ingots. In 2005, I organized a group of divers from England that researched the wreck of the *T.W. Lawson* with me in 2000 to come to Scituate and assist Tom Mulloy's team. Over the course of four days of diving on the wreck, we brought many concretions up to the surface. We also set up a series of volunteer groups, mostly students, to process the material. Although these concretions were extremely difficult to process, we were able to retrieve more porcelain, chains and hardware, but no more ingots.

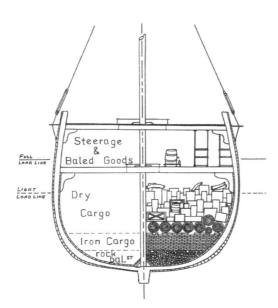

Loading diagram of a ship similar to the *Forest Queen*. *Courtesy Tom Mulloy.*

Diagram of the debris field
140 years after the *Forest Queen*
grounded. *Courtesy Tom Mulloy.*

We did, however, remove shavings from the first ingot Tom found and
had it tested at the University of Devon in southwest England. On May 18,
2005, we received results that confirm that the ingots were not silver but
tin. This was quite a surprise as prior research on the Chinese characters
embossed on the ingot indicated it was a precious metal, most likely silver.

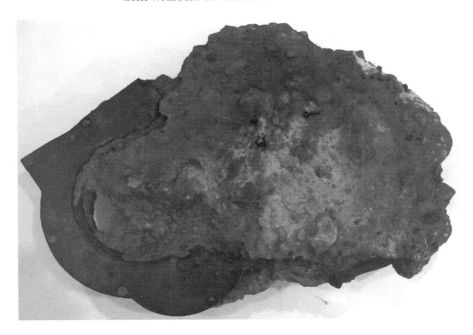

This page: Divers bring up concreted pieces of the wreck that look promising. In this case, the piece above contains part of a porthole. It is then processed by gently chipping away with a blunt object. You can see what is inside the concretion prior to processing with an x-ray image, left, which clearly shows nails and other metals inside. *X-ray courtesy of the United States Navy.*

The ingots contained four distinct markings, with the first meaning "house," the second designating from which time period the ingot was from and the third an "imperial decree" that certifies the authenticity of the piece of metal. These symbols together meant "The Great House of Hsien-Feng, under the Imperial Decree."

Since one of the largest silver foundries in Changsha was the only foundry that had the Imperial Decree during the Hsien-Feng period from 1851 to 1862, a reasonable assumption was that the ingots were silver. Moreover, there are English letters on the back that have a direct relation to trade during this time period. The letter L was determined to mean the Likin Tax, which was regulated by the Imperial Duty, a British Council tax issued for all goods not intended for British ports. A number seventy-three represents the weight of the ingot. The final English phrase shows "WHUC," which stands for Whuchow (or WuZhou in the modern spelling). This was another British system that made sure all goods were of certain quality. In the Far East, the *Forest Queen*'s main commerce was trading opium to the Chinese for porcelain, silk and a myriad of other Chinese goods popular with Americans at the time. The typical trade route was to pick up

The first ingot recovered by Tom Mulloy in 1991.

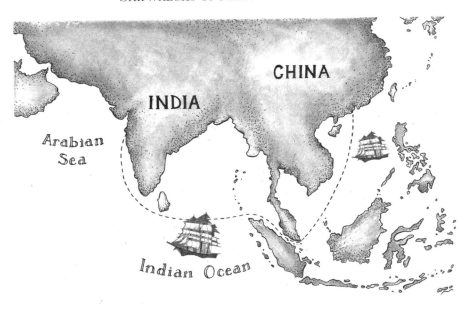

A depiction of a trade route to China used by the *Forest Queen*. *Michelle Garcia, illustrator.*

opium in India, sell it to the Chinese outside of Hong Kong for precious metal, use that precious metal to buy Chinese goods and, when the ship was full, head home. The most common precious metal used in the opium trade was silver.

If the ingots the *Forest Queen* had in her holds were supposed to be silver, there is a mystery here. It could be that the ingots were received as payment in silver and marked that way, even though they were of inferior quality, containing rocks, filler and or some other metal like tin. It would not be surprising that people in the illicit drug trade were less than honorable. To guard against this, most ships had chemists that could test the quality of the opium and the purity of the silver. In fact, additional tests on the ingot conducted locally in 2008 indicated the ingots were coated with silver but were primarily tin.

Another possibility is that the ingots that left China were indeed silver but were swapped out for tin when the *Forest Queen* arrived outside London or while being repaired in Queenstown. It would not have been hard to get tin, as the southwest areas of Devon and Cornwall have historically been rich in this metal. Moreover, it would not have been hard to make a mold of the ingot and its characteristic markings. Another scenario is that the ingots were tin, and this was known and accepted by the captain of the *Forest Queen*.

Tin was a valuable metal and a widely used type of currency. Collecting and selling tin, as well as silver, would have still benefited Daniel Ward and given him the means to start the Irish Mossing fleet and move to a bigger house on First Cliff.

In the end, it may be that whatever precious metal the *Forest Queen* received was not carried back in large quantities and most likely not the twelve tons reported. The process would go something like this: Opium would be sold yearly at auction in India, where it was bought by what by what was called "country firms"—the British, Persian and sometimes American outfits that traded Indian goods with China by arrangement with the East India Company. The only condition was that the country firms sell their opium in Canton (or GuangZhou in the modern spelling) for a precious metal, like silver. However, firms were spared the perilous job of transporting bullion by applying as much of their silver from Canton against their bills in London. Thus a ship like the *Forest Queen* was able to collect silver in payment for its opium in China, only to turn around and pay for its silk, porcelain and other goods bound for American with the same silver. The silver circulated, to be sure, but it also stayed where it was.

One last aspect of this story bears telling. We know that on her way home, the *Forest Queen* stopped in Cobh, Ireland, a seaport town on the south coast of County Cork, to pick up forty-five Irish immigrants. Interestingly, Cobh was renamed Queenstown in 1849 to commemorate a visit by Queen Victoria before being named Cobh again in 1922. In 1853, the potato famine was still raging throughout Ireland; these immigrants, some entire families, were desperate for a new life in Boston, just like the Irish aboard the *St. John* were four years earlier. Fortunately, the passengers on the *Forest Queen* had a happier ending.

When the ship grounded in fairly shallow water off Third Cliff, it remained intact for several days. Onshore, a rescue team quickly sprang to action and brought each passenger safely to the beach—all survived. Although cold and wet, the crew and passengers were no doubt grateful to be on dry land and soon in the warm homes opened up to them by the citizens of Scituate. We see this generosity all along the coast of Mass Bay whenever disaster strikes, for example, with the crew of the *Etrusco* when it grounded in 1956 and to the travelers stranded both at sea and on the roads all around Massachusetts during the Blizzard of '78.

An interesting question is what happened to the forty-five Irish immigrants? After coming ashore and recovering with local families, many of whom were Irish, quite possibly from the same county, did any of them stay? Is it possible

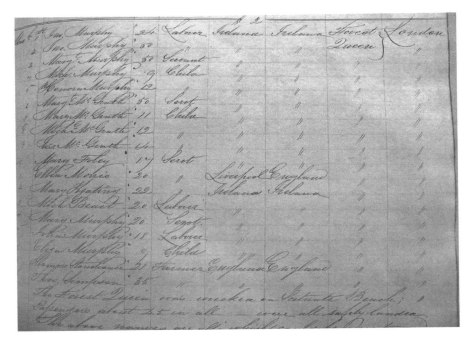

Manifest of *Forest Queen* grounding in 1853. *Courtesy Massachusetts Archives.*

that some stayed, had families and are the great-grandfathers or great-grandmothers of residents of Mass Bay today? To address this question, we have been searching for information on these Irish immigrants. We got a break in 2012 when the manifest was discovered at the Massachusetts Archives. Only eighteen of the forty-five immigrants' names are listed along with their occupations and ages. Unfortunately, their specific home counties in Ireland are not listed:

Name	Age	Occupation
James (?) Murphy	24	Laborer
James (?) Murphy	50	Laborer
Mary Murphy	50	Servant
Michael Murphy	9	Child
Conor (?) Murphy	12	Child

Forest Queen

Name	Age	Occupation
Mary McGrath	50	Servant
Mary McGrath	11	Child
Michael McGrath	12	Child
James McGrath	14	Child
Mary Foley	17	Servant
Ellen Morris	20	Servant
Mary Keating	22	Servant
Michael Benet	20	Laborer
Mary Murphy	20	Servant
John Murphy	18	Laborer
Eliza Murphy	0	Child
Thomas Standhouse	21	Farmer
Thomas Simpson	35	Farmer

Question marks are placed next to some names not written clearly enough to know for sure. "James" Murphy could be "John." "Conor" Murphy could be "Lenore." Also, Eliza Murphy is listed with an age of zero, most likely because she was a newborn. The manifest closes with this statement: "The *Forest Queen* was wrecked on Scituate Beach; passengers about 45 in all were safely landed. The above names are all which could be ascertained." We could also ascertain that, at least with these Irish immigrants looking for a better life, this wreck ended well.

ABOUT THE AUTHOR

Thomas Hall grew up in Scituate, south of Boston, along the coast of Massachusetts Bay. He is an avid wreck diver and historian. In 2000, he was featured in a BBC documentary on the wreck of the *T.W. Lawson*, the world's only seven-masted schooner. His book on this subject was published in 2003. In the past five years, he has  focused his research and dives on wrecks around Massachusetts Bay and lectures extensively on this subject. Tom served in the U.S. Navy in Japan and is a trustee with the Scituate Maritime and Mossing Museum.

As Tom Hall eloquently points out, the history of shipwrecks fascinates us because such a thin line separates us from disaster in so many aspects of life. Here in Massachusetts Bay, many great vessels came to an end, and Tom's moving descriptions offer insight into that thin line. A great read!

William E. Bemis
Kingbury Directory of Shoals Marine Laboratory,
Isles of Shoals

A comprehensive, fresh account of eight historic shipwrecks in Mass Bay, Shipwrecks of Massachusetts Bay *is well-researched and thoughtfully written. Hall offers updated research coupled with insight into how weather, ship's design and human error can merge with disastrous result. Readers of Maritime History will find* Shipwrecks of Massachusetts Bay *an intriguing, excellent reference on wrecks within the Mass Bay.*

Peg Patten
Front Street Book Shop, Scituate